editor's note

日本語を英語に翻訳するにあたり、いくつか留意した点があります。
英語的視点ではわかりにくい部分もあるかもしれませんが、著者の日本語的視点を忠実に伝えたいという思いから、あえて、日本語のリズムや文章の特長を生かして訳しました。

本書は、そもそも、著者が旅の最中に書いていたメモ・日記をもとに作成したものです。
時制や代名詞など、英語的に見れば、文法的に間違っている部分も、その時の臨場感を活かしたいという思いから、あえて、日本語の原文をそのまま伝わるカタチで翻訳してあります。

また、英語に直訳できないもの、日本語でしか表現できないものについても、脚注もつけず、作品の持つ全体のトーンやフィーリングを大事にしたいという思いから、あえて、英語での余計な説明を加えておりません。

When translating this book from Japanese into English, a few points were kept in mind. There may be parts difficult to understand from an English viewpoint, but wanting to faithfully convey the author's Japanese viewpoint, the translation deliberately utilizes the strengths of the writing style and rhythm of the Japanese language.

This book was created from what began as notes and journals the author recorded while traveling. From an English viewpoint, the grammatical errors, such as tenses and pronouns, are deliberately translated to convey the Japanese original as is, in hopes that the reader will sense the reality of the writing.

In addition, for those words that cannot be directly translated into English or can only be expressed in Japanese, footnotes were not added to preserve the general tone and feeling of this work. In doing so, additional explanations in English are not included.

はじめに

1998年11月から2000年7月にかけて、約1年8ヶ月間。
結婚したばかりの妻とふたりで、気の向くままに世界数十ヶ国の路上を歩いた。

自分は、3年間続けた会社を離れてフリーになったばかりだったし、銀座のOLだった妻のさやかは、寿退社をしたばかりで、長い旅に出るには、「今しかない!」という絶好のタイミングだった。

旅のコースも、期間も、特に決めなかった。
「スタートはオーストラリア。あとは気の向くままに。まぁ、金がなくなったら帰ろう」
それだけを決めて出発した。

世界中の路上で、カフェで、ビーチで、バス停で、安宿のベッドで....
大好きなコーラを片手に、タバコを吹かしながら、
自分の「ココロの井戸」を掘るようにして、いくつもの詩を書いた。

「いいじゃん!」と感じるシーンに出逢うたびに、
ポケットから小さなデジカメを取り出して、何千枚もの写真を撮った。

帰国後、旅中に残した詩と写真の中から、特に気に入ったものだけを選んで、1冊にまとめたら、この本が出来上がった。

オーストラリア、東南アジア、ユーラシア、ヨーロッパ、アフリカ、南米、北米、日本....
世界の路上の片隅で、さまざまな人々が僕にくれた「LOVE&FREE」のカケラを、あなたに贈ります。

高橋　歩

Forward

From November, 1998, through July, 2000; for approximately one year and eight months, just married, my wife and I walked the streets of thirty-some countries of the world, traveling in any direction our hearts desired.

I had just resigned from a company I started and managed for three years.
My wife, Sayaka, who worked as an "OL" (office lady) in Ginza, Tokyo, had just resigned from her job to marry me, and the timing was perfect to take a long vacation. It was "Now or Never"!

We didn't particularly plan out "where", "how", or "for how long". "Let's start in Australia. And the rest, we'll play it by ear. And hey, we'll just come back when we run out of money." That was all we decided, and we were off.

On the streets of the world, in various cafes, on beaches, at bus stops, and in bed at hostels...
With my favorite Coke in one hand, smoking a cigarette, digging deep into the bottom of my heart and soul, I wrote a bunch of poems.

When I came across scenes that felt "great!", I reached for the tiny digital camera in my pocket, and took thousands of photos.

After returning from our world journey, I gathered the notes and photos I especially liked, put them together, and this book came to life.

Australia, Southeast Asia, Eurasia, Europe, Africa, South America, North America, and Japan...
I give to you, fragments of "Love & Free" that many different people gave me from all corners of the various streets of our world.

Ayumu Takahashi

ALASKA

GREAT BRITAIN

CALIFORNIA

SPAIN

WAI

MOROCC

TAHITI

PERU

EASTER ISLAND

ANTARCT

INLAND
AMSTERDAM
PARIS
RUSSIA
MONGOLIA
TOKYO
ISRAEL
NEPAL
EGYPT
INDIA
THAILAND
THE PHILIPPINES
MALAYSIA
KENYA
SINGAPORE
BALI
AUSTR
MAURITIUS

目 次

オーストラリアへ

東南アジアへ

ユーラシアへ

ヨーロッパへ

アフリカへ

南米＆北米へ

日本へ

CONTENTS :

Journey 1 :
to AUSTRALIA

Journey 2 :
to SOUTH-EAST ASIA

Journey 3 :
to EURASIA

Journey 4 :
to EUROPE

Journey 5 :
to AFRICA

Journey 6 :
to SOUTH&NORTH AMERICA

Journey Final :
to JAPAN

Journey 1 :

Aust

ralia

キミの心の中のトムソーヤは元気かい？

How's the Tom Sawyer in you?

Weekly Life

各地で「ホリデーアパートメント」（安い貸別荘のようなもの）に１週間ずつ泊まりながら旅を続けている。

地球上のあらゆる場所で、「１週間の暮らし」を味わう。

まるで、１週間ごとに引っ越しをしているみたいだ。

一面の海、古びた駐車場、隣のビルの壁、高層ビル街の夜景、緑溢れる公園....
部屋の窓から見える景色が、１週間ごとに変わるっていうのは、とってもイカしている。

どこの街に行っても、
免税店、観光案内所、空港というよりは、
スーパーマーケット、地元のBAR、バス・ストップなどに足が向く。

お金には少々制約があるが、時間だけは無限にある旅。

日本で頑張っているであろう仲間達への懐かしさと、
新しく出逢うであろう見知らぬ人々への期待が、胸の中で行ったり来たりしてる。

大好きな彼女とタバコと酒、そしてホンの少しの運さえあれば、当分は楽しくやっていけそうな気がする。

Weekly life

We stay in "holiday apartments" (cheap vacation houses)
at each place one week at a time, and continue our journey.

We get a taste of "One week in the life of..."
in various places on this Earth.

It's almost like moving every week.

The entire ocean; an old, run-down parking lot; the
wall of the building next door; the night view of a
skyscraper city; a park of overflowing greenery...
The scenery from our window changes once a week.
Cool!

In every town
Instead of the duty free shops,
tourist information centers, or airports
I find myself going to the supermarkets,
the local bars, or the bus stops.

A journey with limited money, but unlimited time.

Memories of my friends doing their best towards
their dreams back home in Japan and at the same time
Expectations of the new people I am sure to meet
My feelings go back and forth in my heart.

The woman I love, smokes, and some booze,
and just a little bit of luck
With just that for the time being,
I think I can enjoy myself.

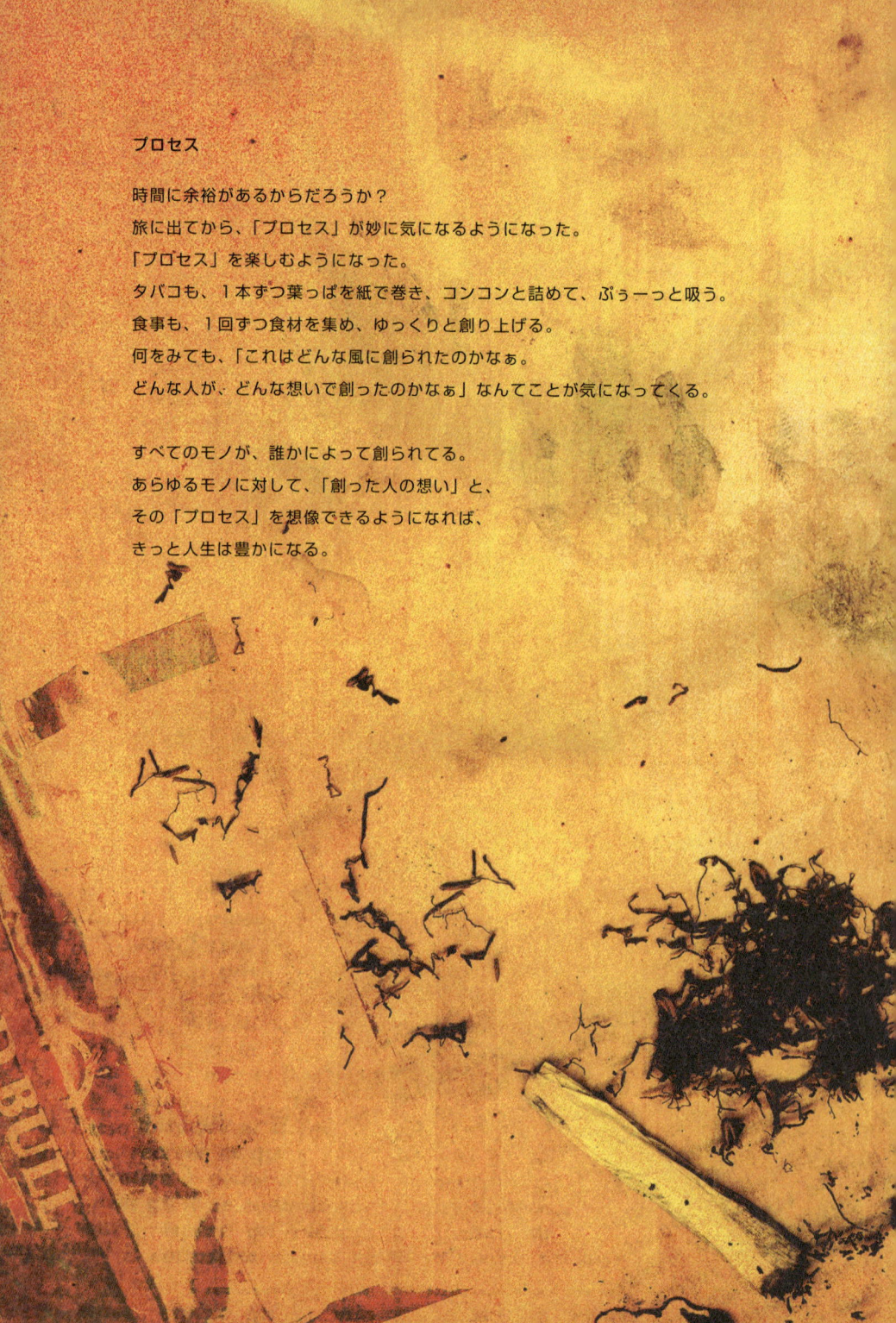

プロセス

時間に余裕があるからだろうか?
旅に出てから、「プロセス」が妙に気になるようになった。
「プロセス」を楽しむようになった。
タバコも、1本ずつ葉っぱを紙で巻き、コンコンと詰めて、ぷぅーっと吸う。
食事も、1回ずつ食材を集め、ゆっくりと創り上げる。
何をみても、「これはどんな風に創られたのかなぁ。
どんな人が、どんな想いで創ったのかなぁ」なんてことが気になってくる。

すべてのモノが、誰かによって創られてる。
あらゆるモノに対して、「創った人の想い」と、
その「プロセス」を想像できるようになれば、
きっと人生は豊かになる。

Process

Maybe it's because I have free time on my hands?
Since this journey began, I have become unusually
interested in the "PROCESS".
I've come to enjoy the "PROCESS".
Cigarettes for example, I roll the leaves with paper,
one by one, tap it to pack it in, and then smoke it.
Each meal starts by going out and finding each
ingredient, and taking time to prepare it.
Anything I see, I find myself wondering things like,
"How is this made? Who made it? And what thoughts
did he have in making it?"

Everything is created by somebody.
If one could learn to imagine, in any given thing,
the "creator's thoughts" and the "process",
it might lead to a better life.

昨日、見たもの

昨日、街のメインストリートをパンイチ（白いパンツ一枚）で歌いながら歩いているおっさんを見た。
昨日、ビーチで70才くらいの老婆と若い男のカップルがディープキスしているのを見た。
昨日、混んでいるスーパーマーケットの床で熟睡しているアボリジニの少年を見た。
昨日、真っ昼間の公園の芝生でエッチしているふたりを見た。
昨日、めちゃめちゃ陽気でポップな浮浪者に逢った。
昨日、顔面にハエを30匹くらいくっつけてニコニコしているおばさんを見た。
昨日、「GOOD MORNING!」って言いながら、起きた瞬間にビールを一気飲みした奴がいた。
昨日、「死ぬのって楽しみだよね、気持ちいいらしいよ！」ってハイテンションで語るおじさんに逢った。

いいねぇ。愉快だね。

What I Saw Yesterday

Yesterday, I saw a man wearing only white underpants
walking and singing down Main Street
Yesterday, at the beach, I saw an old woman in her 70s
embraced in a deep kiss with a young man
Yesterday, I saw a young Aborigine boy sound asleep
on the floor of a busy supermarket
Yesterday, I saw a couple making love on the lawn
of the park in broad daylight
Yesterday, I met an overly cheerful and "POP" bum
Yesterday, I saw a lady that was all smiles, with 30
or so flies on her face
Yesterday, I saw a guy wake up, say, "Good morning!",
and without missing a beat, down a beer
Yesterday, I met a man that excitedly told me,
"I'm looking forward to dying. I hear it feels goooood!"

Life is wonderful!

A PUNTE

Lowe
chief,
orise s
Advert
his ant
so imp
"swimt
pelled
With
Inge fo
two
but fel
Barclay
Eclipse
So the
waters

named Summer Cove, watched by a number of ladies checking out their credentials.

Half-way out, Barclay's undies

jumper to collect the agency's nine accolades. His attire attracted much hilarity, particularly from the compere (the Irish comedian,

More Kinsale gossip

TBWA/GGT Simons Palmer's team chose some unusual accommodation for their stay in Kinsale — namely a pig farm. While we can't confirm that it was a genuine pig farm, a lot of TBWA's normally bacon-friendly creatives were

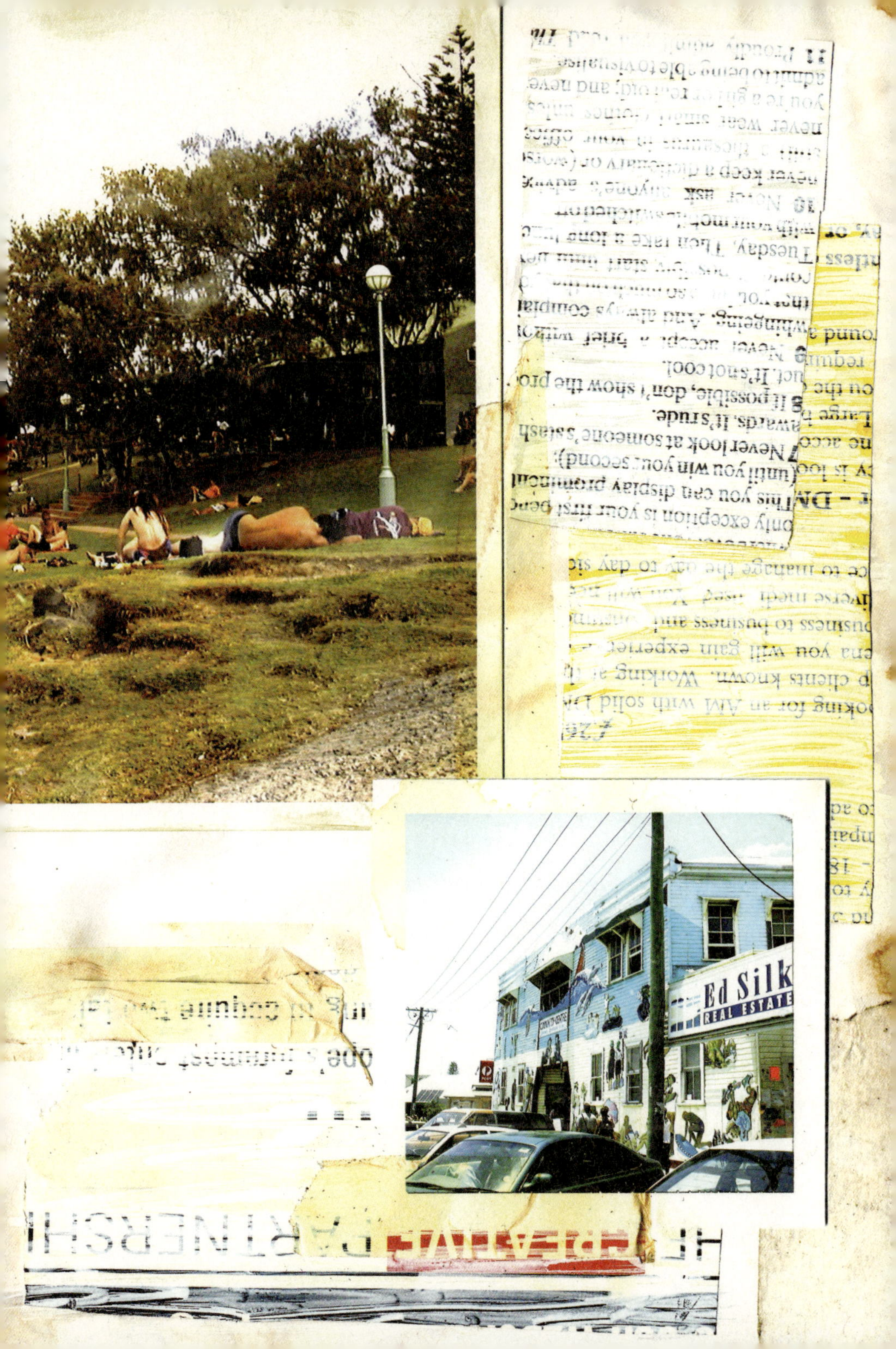

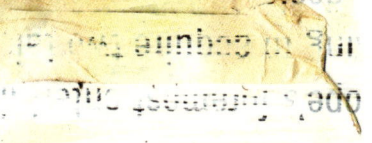

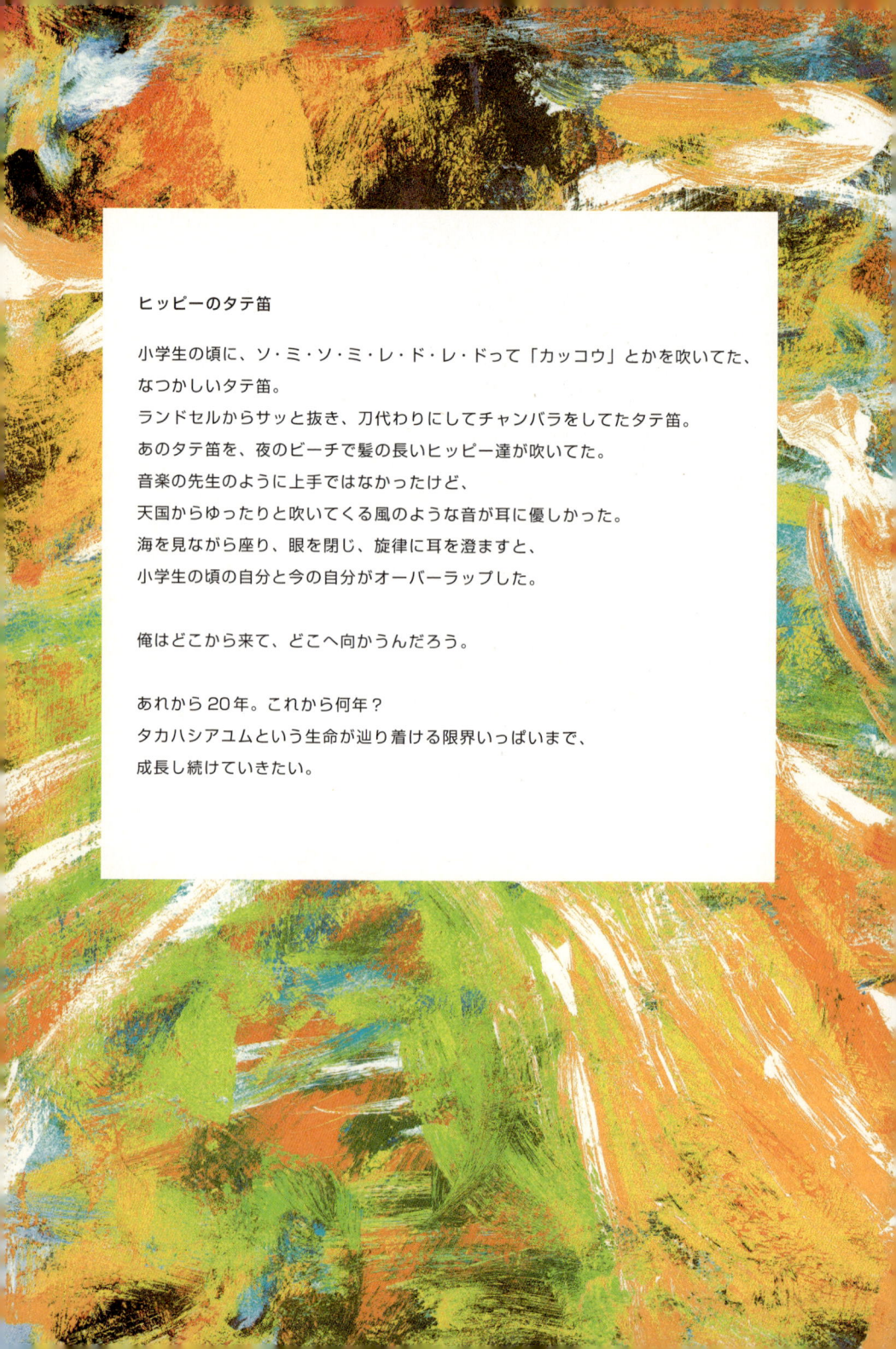

ヒッピーのタテ笛

小学生の頃に、ソ・ミ・ソ・ミ・レ・ド・レ・ドって「カッコウ」とか吹いてた、
なつかしいタテ笛。
ランドセルからサッと抜き、刀代わりにしてチャンバラをしてたタテ笛。
あのタテ笛を、夜のビーチで髪の長いヒッピー達が吹いてた。
音楽の先生のように上手ではなかったけど、
天国からゆったりと吹いてくる風のような音が耳に優しかった。
海を見ながら座り、眼を閉じ、旋律に耳を澄ますと、
小学生の頃の自分と今の自分がオーバーラップした。

俺はどこから来て、どこへ向かうんだろう。

あれから20年。これから何年？
タカハシアユムという生命が辿り着ける限界いっぱいまで、
成長し続けていきたい。

Hippie's Recorder

The recorder
brings back memories of elementary school
practicing how to play
so-mi-so-mi-re-do-re-do or "Cuckoo"
pulling it out of my schoolbag and pretending it
to be a sword in battles with my friends
At night on the beach
long-haired hippies were playing that recorder
They weren't as good as my music teacher
but the sound like a wind blowing softly from heaven
was gentle to the ear
Sitting and watching the ocean
closing my eyes
and concentrating on listening
I felt as if my elementary school
self and present self had overlapped

Where did I come from, and where am I going?
It's been twenty years since then.
How many years from now?
I will keep growing the life of Ayumu Takahashi
to its fullest potential.

長距離バスの旅で発見した法則 1

イタリア人：ハエに弱い。
アメリカ人：狭い場所に弱い。
中　国　人：孤独に弱い。

長距離バスの旅で発見した法則 2

「NO FOOD」〜食べ物禁止のバスにて〜

日　本　人：コソコソ食べる。しばらくして見つかって注意される。やめる。
アメリカ人：堂々と食べる。すぐに見つかって注意される。やめる。
アボリジニ：堂々と食べる。すぐに見つかって注意される。
　　　　　　それでも食べ続ける。

Laws Discovered on Long-Distance Buses - Part 1

Italians: weak against flies
Americans: weak against small spaces
Chinese: weak against solitude

Laws Discovered on Long-Distance Buses - Part 2

"NO FOOD" -- *On buses that prohibit eating
Japanese: eats on the sly, trying not to get caught,
             gets caught after a while and is warned,
             quits eating
Americans: eats confidently without hiding it,
             gets caught immediately and is warned,
             quits eating
Aborigines: eats confidently without hiding it,
             gets caught immediately and is warned,
             continues eating

表現者として

万人のハートを軽くなでるのではなく、
ひとりのハートに、ぐさりと突き刺さる表現がしたい。

顔の見えない大勢の人に向かって、受け取りやすいスローボールを投げるより、
そこにいるアナタに向けて、まっすぐな超豪速球を投げたい。

普遍的な作品を創り上げミリオンセラーを飛ばしたい、という欲求は当然あるが、
コムロのような普遍性ではなく、レノンのような普遍性を求めたい。

「ひとり」に対する深く強烈なオモイをつきつめることでたどり着いた「ココロ
の奥のほうにあるアッタカイモノ」で、多くの人とつながりたい。

人間のココロに棲んでいるアッタカイモノだけは、
今も昔も、東洋も西洋も、本質的には変わらないと思うから。

As an Artist

Instead of lightly touching the hearts of millions
I'd rather express myself so that it stabs into the
heart of one

Instead of tossing an easy-to-catch, slow-ball to
a bunch of faces I can't even make out
I'd rather throw a straight, super-fast-ball
directly to you, right there

Naturally, I have a desire to create a universal
piece that becomes a MILLION SELLER
but instead of the universality of KOMURO,
I seek the universality of LENNON

Probing into the deep, strong thoughts for "one"
and working your way to that
"warm and fuzzy feeling deep down inside the heart"
I want to connect to many people in this way

because in the past and in the present
in the East and the West
I believe that "warm and fuzzy feeling" in people's
hearts are essentially the same

小手先の技術はいらない。
大げさな批評や解説もいらない。

生き方がアートだ。

死ぬときに、「自分という作品」に感動したいだけ。

no need for superficial skills
no need for exaggerated reviews or commentaries

LIFESTYLE is an ART!

when I die, I just hope to be moved by "MY LIFE"
as a piece of work

サヤカの喜んだ顔が、好きだ。
ごちゃごちゃ能書きをたれる前に、
まずは、この女性を喜ばせることから始めよう。

I love Sayaka's face when she smiles
before making jumbled statements
I will start by making this woman happy

ふたりがひとつであるために。ふたりがふたりであるために。

for the two of us are one
for the two of us are two

あるワイナリーで

オーストラリアのド田舎で、小さなワイナリーに寄る。

手の不自由そうなおじいちゃんが、一生懸命に、
１粒１粒ブドウを育て、
１滴１滴蒸留し、
１本１本大事に創った赤ワイン。

ガキの頃、弁当のおにぎりにオフクロの味を感じたように、
このワインは、おじいちゃんの味がした。

「今日はおじいちゃんの人生に乾杯しよう！」

心を込めて創った「作品」には、
たとえワイン１本でも、「魂」がこもっている。

At a winery

stopped off at a small winery in the remote
country-side of Australia

an old man that seemed as if he had difficulty
using his hands
working very hard
growing each and every grape
distilling each and every drop
producing preciously
each and every bottle of red wine

like finding "Mom's flavor" in the rice balls
of bentos she made for me as a kid
this wine had "this old man's flavor"

"Today, let's toast to this old man's life!"

pouring one's heart into one's work
even one bottle of wine, is packed with "soul"

ONE WORLD　〜世界はひとつ〜

ジョン・レノンは、「ONE WORLD」という愛を音楽で表現した。

旅先で出逢ったおじさんは「ONE WORLD」という愛を、
世界中の雑貨を集めた小さな雑貨屋さんで表現したという。
「ONE WORLD」と刻まれた店の看板は、とっても地味だけど
手創りの暖かみに溢れていた。

ジョン・レノンも、このおじさんも、俺は同じように好きだ。

愛の表現方法に、ルールなんてない。

ONE WORLD

John Lennon expressed a love, "One World", through music.

A man I met on the road expressed a love through a small shop that sold trinkets from around the world. The shop's sign carved with the words "One World" was really plain, but was overflowing with the warmth of something hand-made.

John Lennon and this man, I love them both the same.

There are no rules to expressing love.

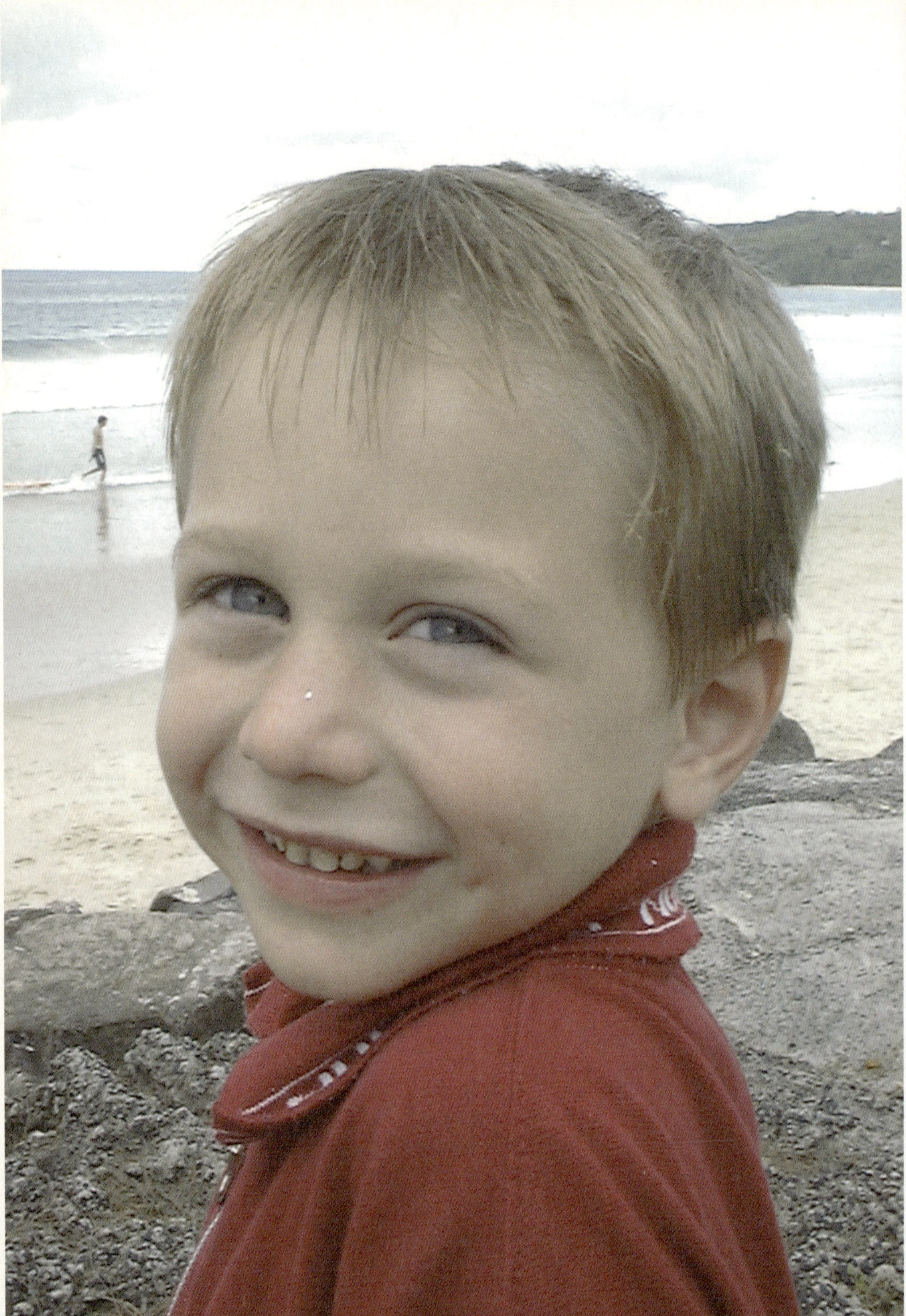

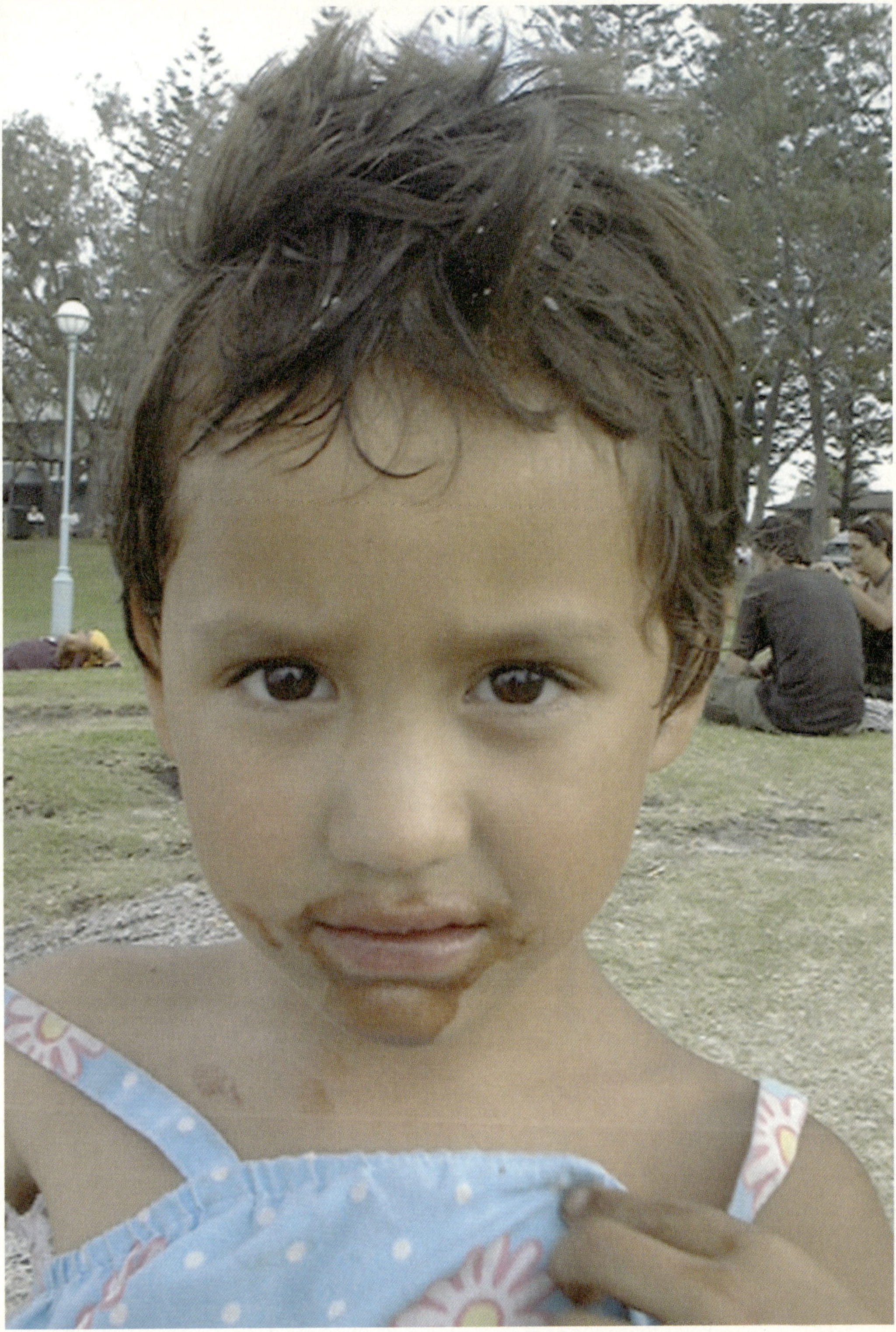

playground

子供の頃、「自転車」を手に入れて、町内すべてが遊び場になった。
ヤンキーの頃、「バイク」を手に入れて、県内すべてが遊び場になった。
そして、今、「時間」を手に入れて、世界すべてを遊び場にしようとしている。

昔から、新しい遊び場で新しい遊びを考えるのが大得意だった。
ノリは全く変わってない。
道具が変わり、年齢とともに遊び場が拡大しているだけのこと。

「ねぇねぇ、何して遊ぼうか？」
この問いほど、俺のクリエイティブを刺激する言葉はない。

ねぇねぇ、何して遊んでる？

playground

As a kid, I got a bicycle
and the entire town became my playground
As a teenage-pank, I got a motorcycle
and the entire prefecture became my playground
And now, I got time
and am trying to make the entire world my playground

I've always been really good at thinking up new ways
to play in new playgrounds
My style hasn't changed at all
The tools have changed with age
my playground just keeps expanding

"Hey, what do you wanna play?"
There aren't any words that could stimulate
my creativity more than this question does.

"Hey, what are you playing?"

たまには窓を開けて、未来の風景を見てるかい？

Once in a while, are you opening your window
to take a look at the future?

ON THE ROAD

道ばたから一生懸命に走る他のランナー達を見て、
歓声を上げたり、感想を言い合ったりするのにも飽きたろ。
スタートラインで戸惑い、最後まで走りきれるかどうかを心配するのも
疲れるだけだ。

そろそろ、道の上に立って自分も走り始めようぜ。
遅くたっていい。疲れたら歩いたっていい。ビリッケツでもいい。
一歩進むごとに、風景は変わっていく。

足踏みしてても、靴の底は減るぜ。

On the Road

Aren't you bored standing on the sidelines
watching others run really hard
cheering them on
and exchanging opinions?
Worrying if you'll be able to finish the race
standing at the start line with uncertainties
is just too tiring

It's time to get up there on the road
and start running
It's OK even if it's slowly
And if it gets tiring, then walking is OK
Coming in last place is OK
With each step, the scenery will change

Even if you run in place
the soles of your shoes are bound to wear out

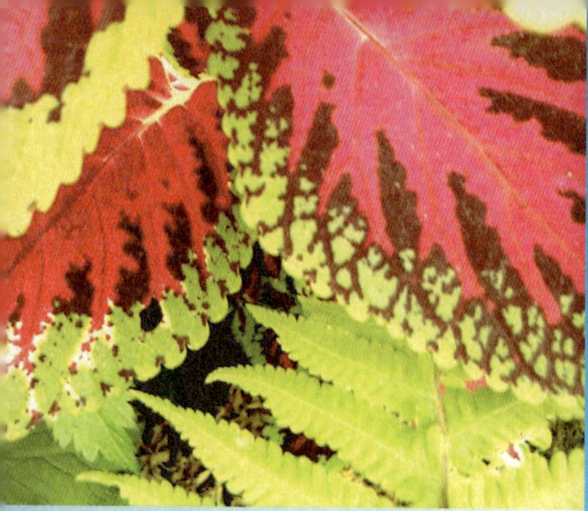
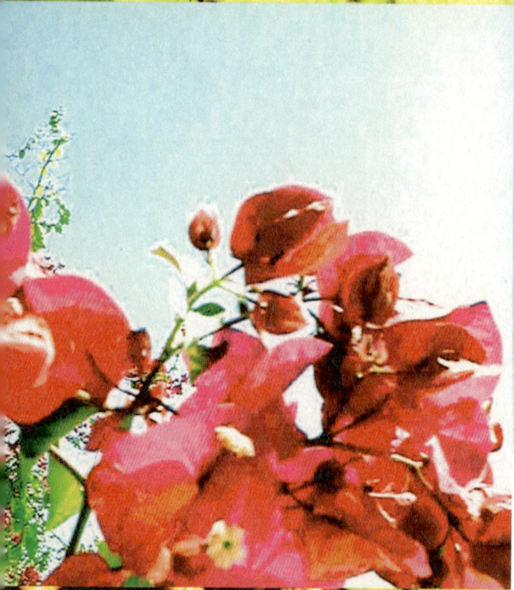
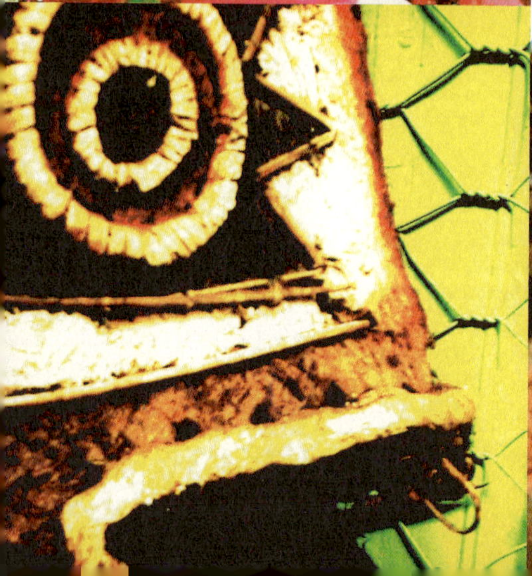

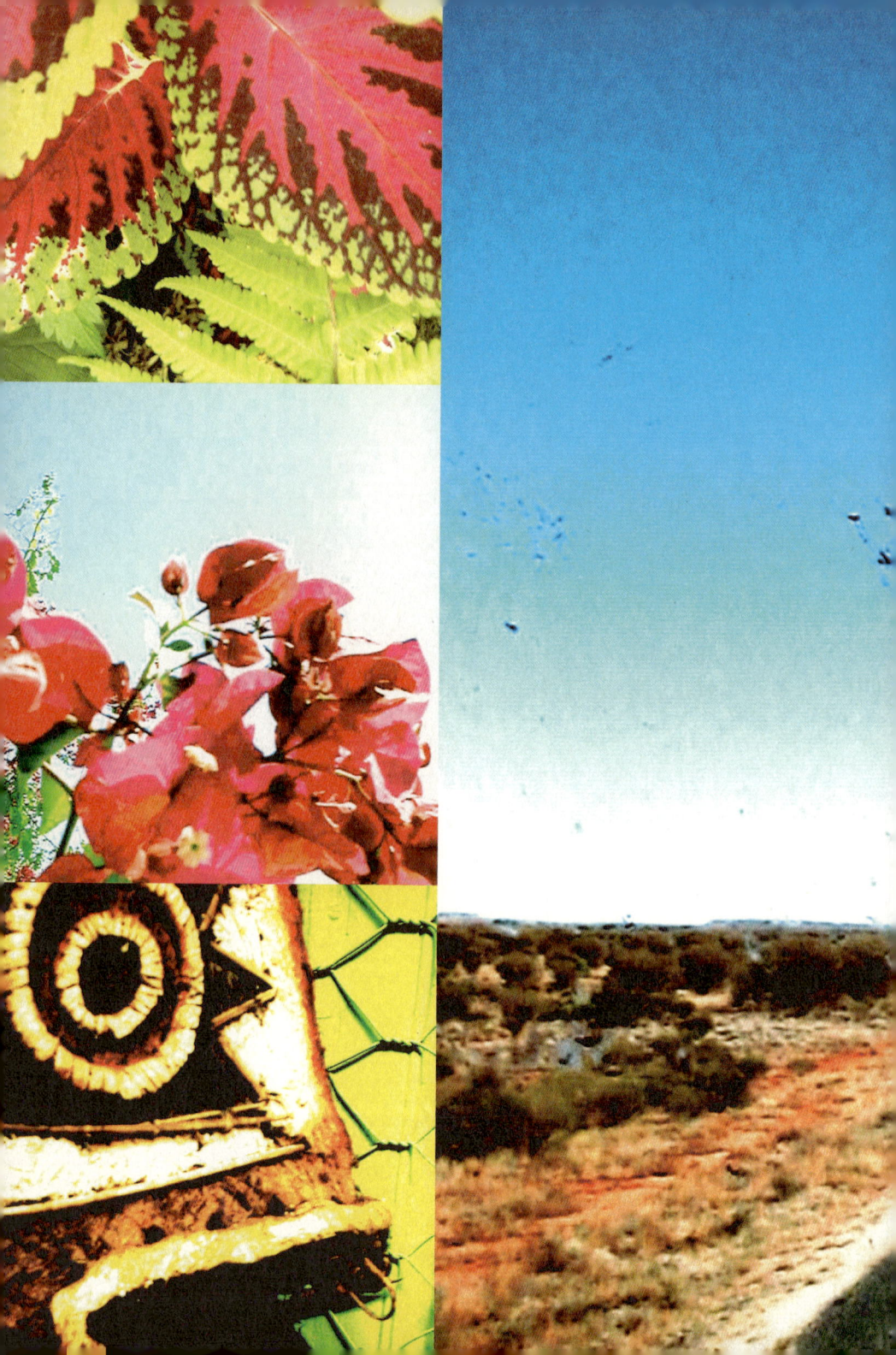

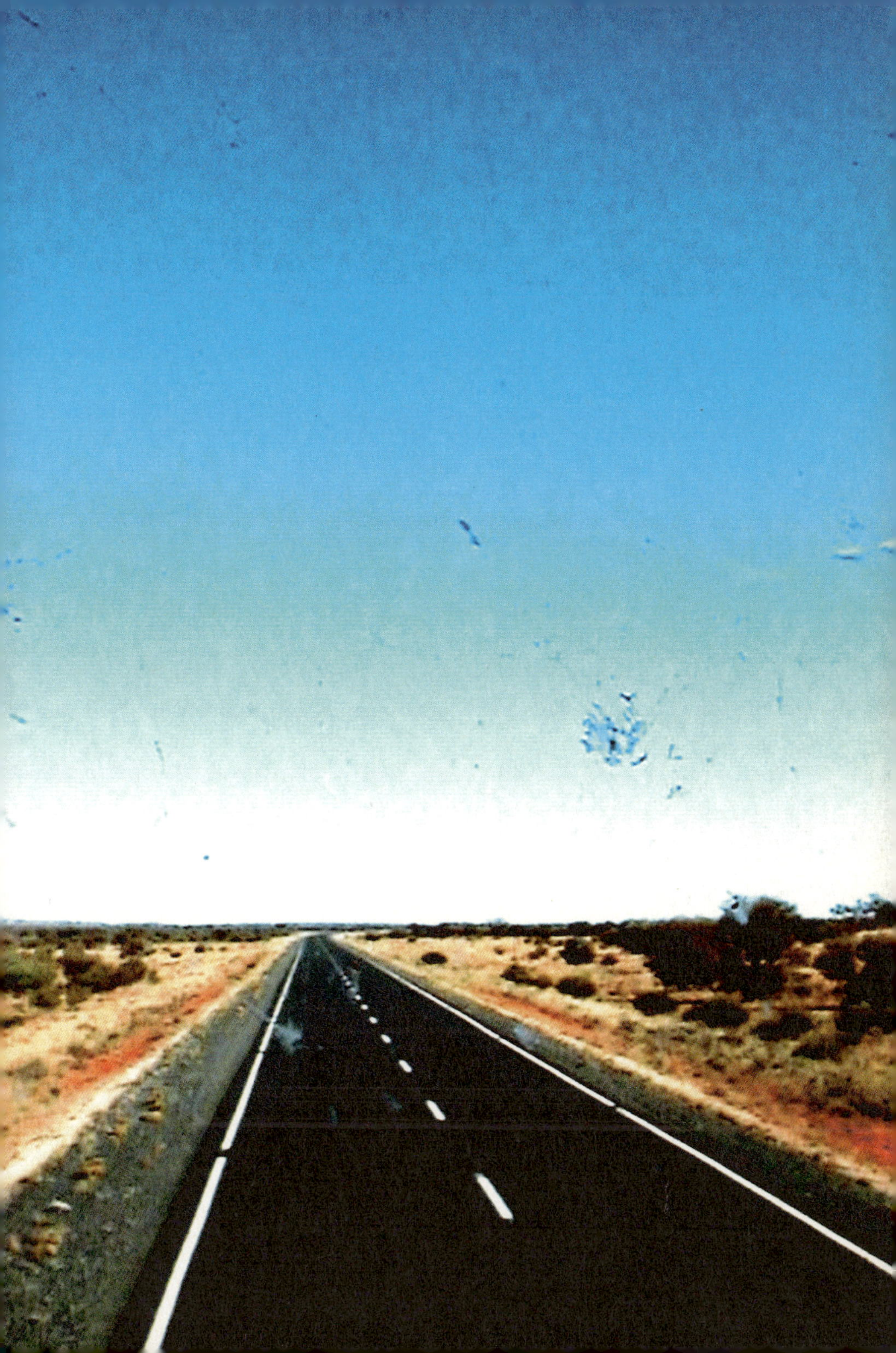

イルカ時間

数年ぶりに、インド洋でイルカに逢った。
相変わらず、イルカっていう生き物は波長がいい。

イルカと一緒に泳ぐと優しい気持ちになれるのは、なぜなんだろう....
イルカと初めて泳いだとき、彼らの優しいオーラに強烈にひかれ、
イルカになりたいとさえ思った。

～イルカのように優しくなるためには、瞑想をし、心を静かにする必要がある～
イルカ人間と呼ばれるジャック・マイヨールの本を読み、
「瞑想」の大切さを感じた。

毎日の忙しい生活の中で、静かな場所で自分の心をイルカにする時間が必要だ、
ということはよくわかったが、部屋の床に座り、眼を閉じて、呼吸を整え....と
いうのが、どうもスタイル的にピンとこなかった。

そこで、俺は俺なりの「瞑想」～高層ビルのカフェでおいしいコーヒーを飲みな
がらぼーっとする～を始めた。最初はなんだか落ち着かなかったが、意識的に通
っているうちにだんだん慣れてきて、そこで過ごす時間が気持ちよくなってきた。
そこにいると、少しだけ優しい気持ちになれるようになった。

どんなに生活が慌ただしくても、「イルカな時間」を確保できるようになったこ
とで、俺は流されるのではなく、流れて生きている実感を得られるようになった。

不思議なことに、たかが「カフェでの30分」によって、
俺は明らかに変わり始めた。

カフェに限らず、気軽に行けて、ひとりっきりで気持ちよくぼーっと出来る「瞑
想スペース」を持つこと。
それは、意外と大きなきっかけになるかもしれない。

Dolphin Time

It's been a few years since I'd seen a dolphin, this time in the Indian Ocean. These beings called dolphins, their vibe is as awesome as ever.

Why is it that I get this gentle feeling just swimming with them? The first time I swam with them, I was strongly pulled into this gentle aura, and seriously wanted to be one of them.

*In order to be gentle as dolphins, there's a need to meditate and quite the heart. Reading the book by the "Dolphin Man", Jacques Mayol, I realized the importance of "meditation".

Within busy everyday lifestyles, I understand the need to take time out in a quiet place to settle myself into a "dolphin state". But, sitting on the floor of my room, closing my eyes, and concentrating on breathing, just didn't quite hit home as "my" style.

So, I came up with my own style of meditation. I started going to a cafe in a high-rise building, drinking good coffee, and thinking about nothing. I was a little antsy in the beginning, but after some time of consciously going, I got used to it, and I became comfortable with the time I spent at the cafe. While there, I was able to feel gentle just for a little bit.

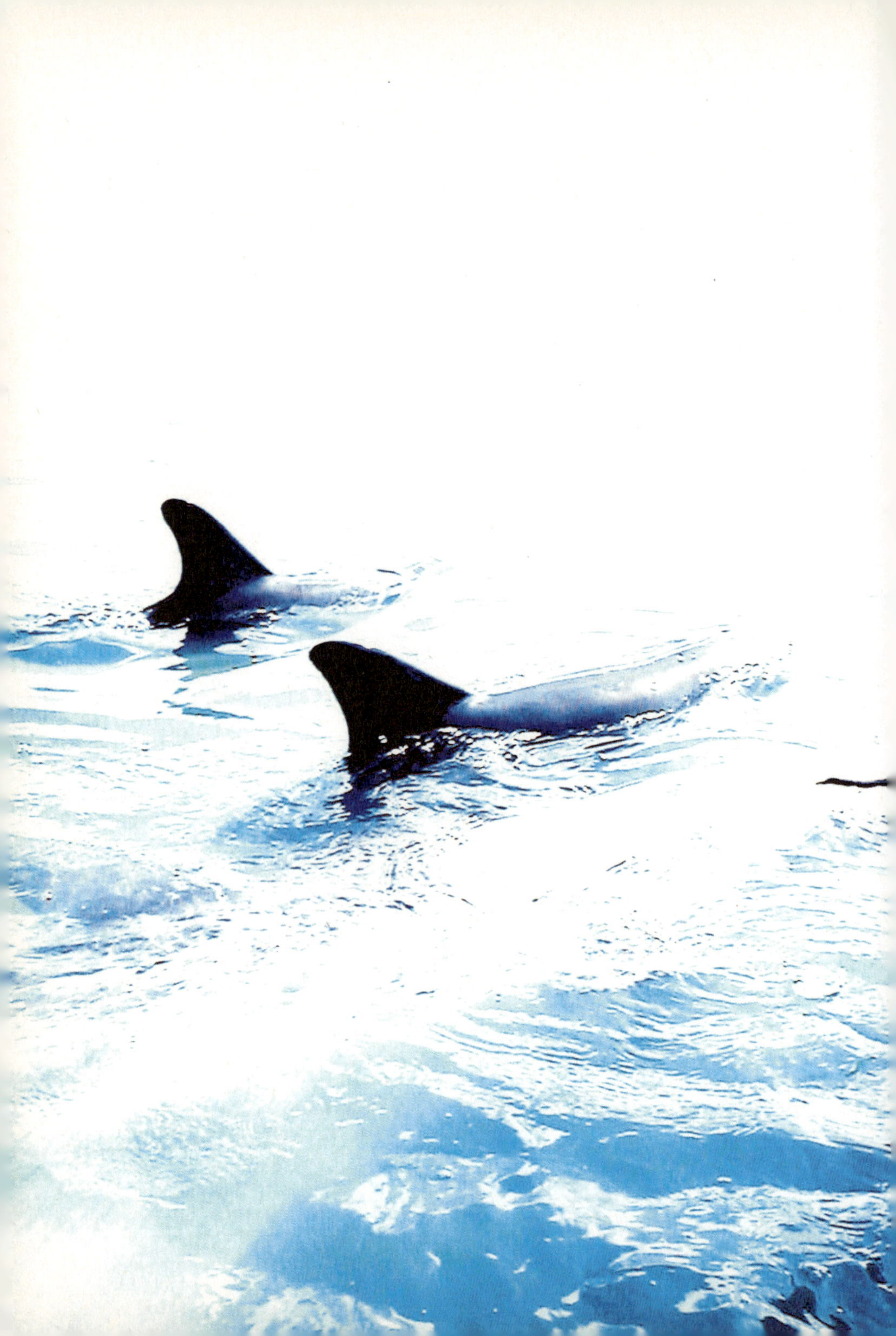

No matter how busy I am, I put aside "Dolphin Time"
for myself, and because of that, I've come to realize
that I am flowing with life, instead of being flushed
through it.

It's strange. It's just "half an hour at a cafe",
but I've clearly started to change.

Not limited to cafes; any place I can easily go,
alone, and think of nothing and relax.
To have my own "meditation space" may bring an
unexpected, big chance.

ゴミ処理場から始まる旅

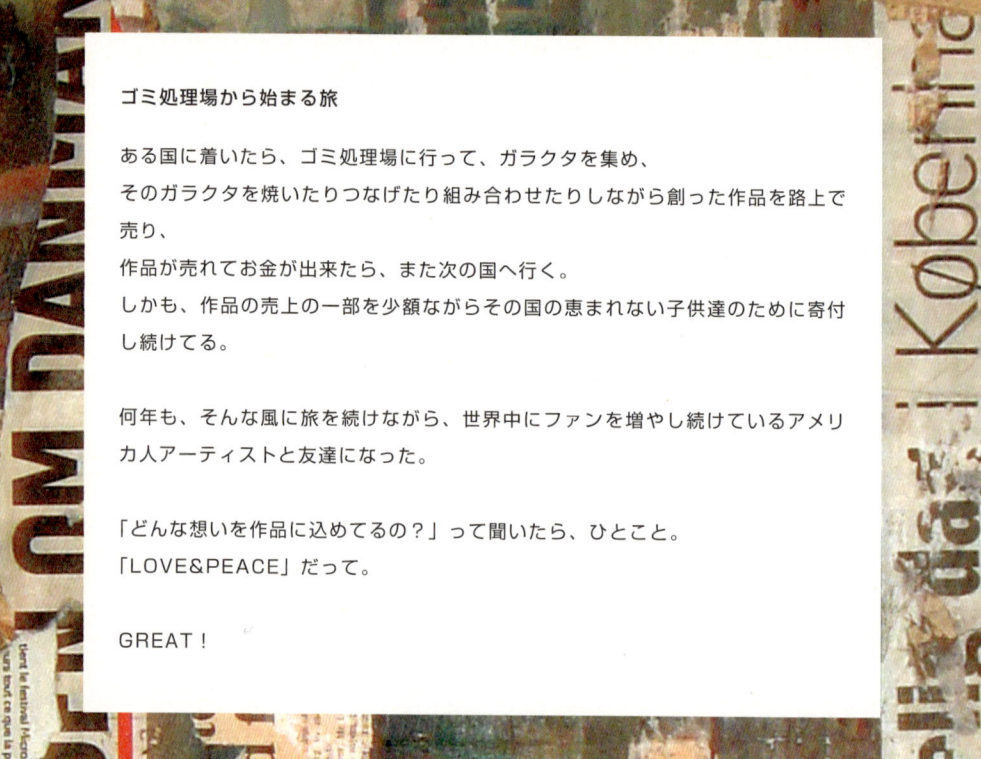

ある国に着いたら、ゴミ処理場に行って、ガラクタを集め、
そのガラクタを焼いたりつなげたり組み合わせたりしながら創った作品を路上で売り、
作品が売れてお金が出来たら、また次の国へ行く。
しかも、作品の売上の一部を少額ながらその国の恵まれない子供達のために寄付し続けてる。

何年も、そんな風に旅を続けながら、世界中にファンを増やし続けているアメリカ人アーティストと友達になった。

「どんな想いを作品に込めてるの？」って聞いたら、ひとこと。
「LOVE&PEACE」だって。

GREAT！

A Trip that Starts from a Junkyard

Arrives in a country, goes to the junkyard,
collects odds and ends, uses the junk to create
an art piece, sells them on the street,
when he's sold enough to make a sum of money,
moves on to the next country. And on top of that,
continues to donate a percentage (however small)
of the sales to the underprivileged children of
each country.

I became friends with this American artist that
has been traveling like this for years, gaining
more and more fans all over the world.

"What thoughts do you put into your work?" I asked.
He says, just one phrase, "Love & Peace".

GREAT!

いつもこころにあおぞらを。あおぞらはつながっている。

KEEP BLUE SKY IN THE HEART.
BLUE SKIES ARE CONNECTED.

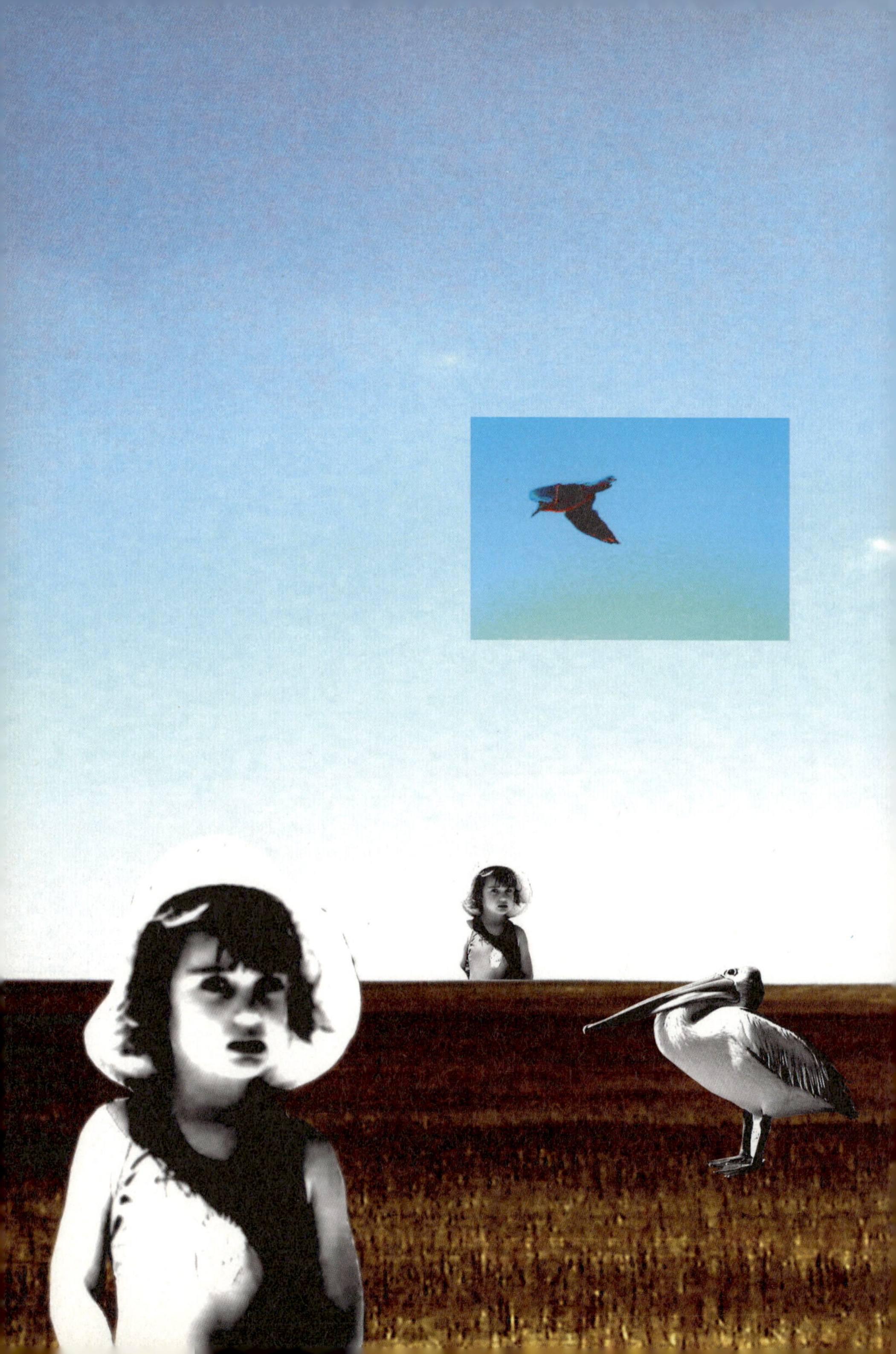

happy

Journey 2 :

South-e

ast Asia

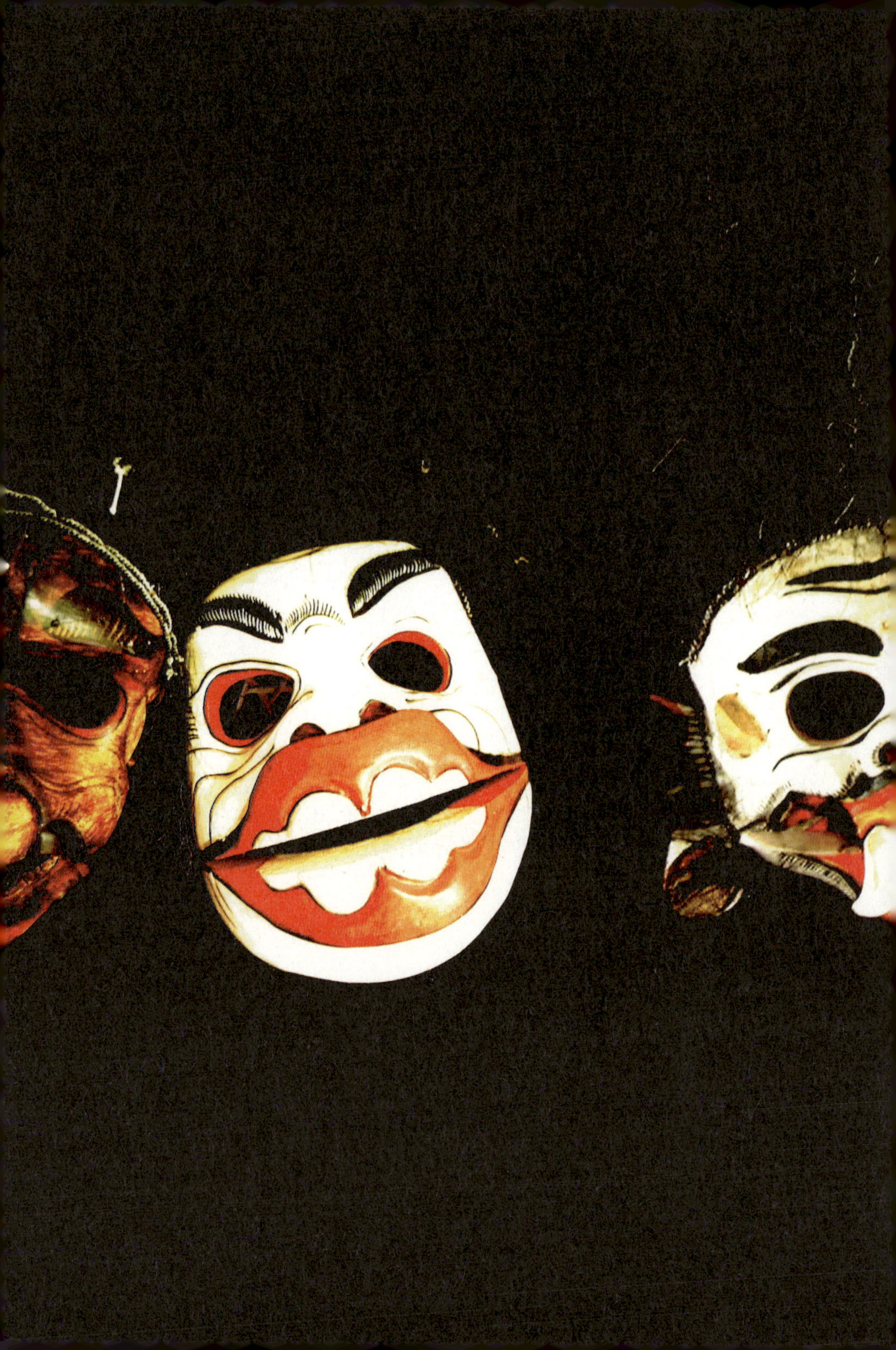

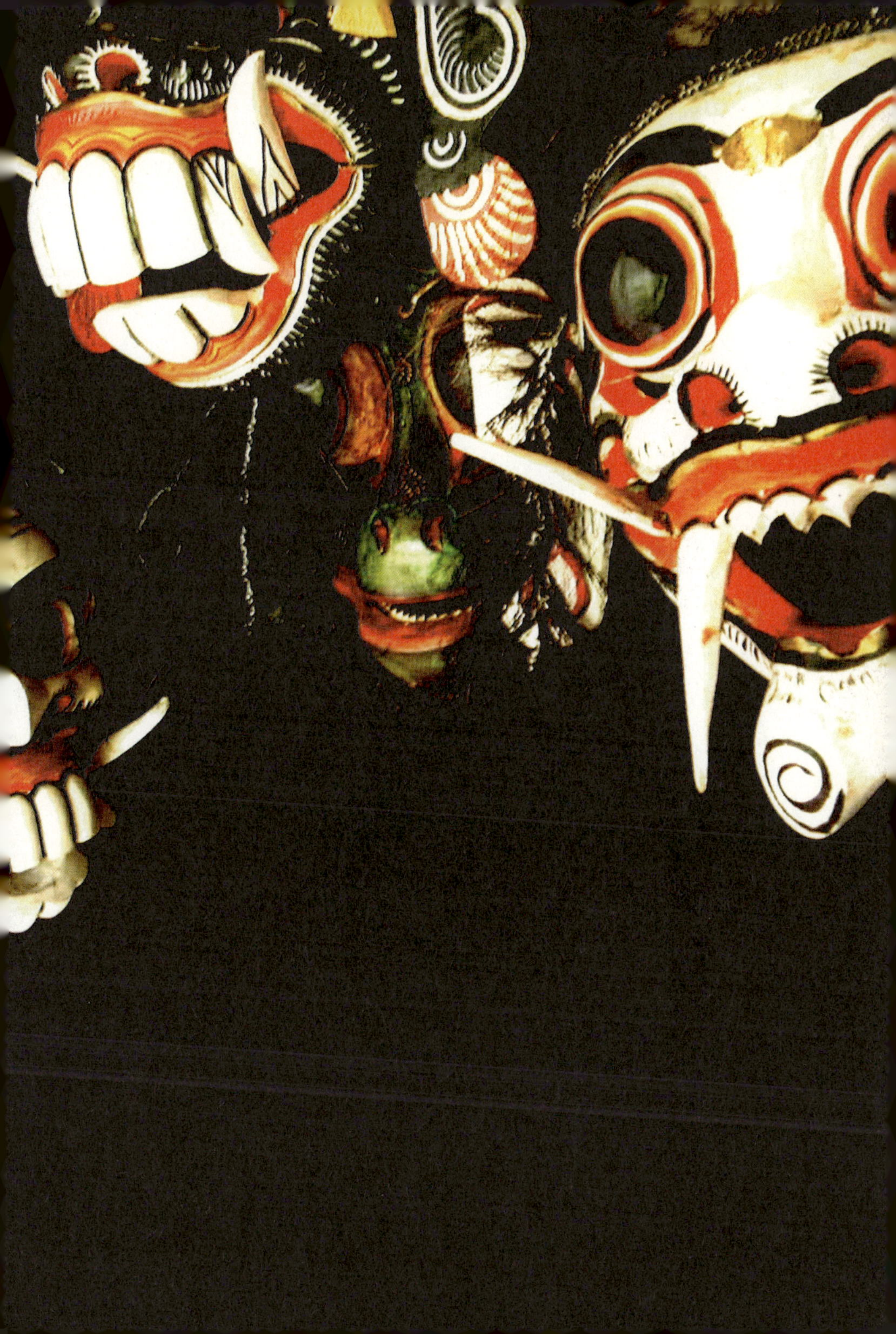

ふたりの自由

俺があくびをすると、80%の可能性で彼女にうつる。
俺がおならをすると、90%の可能性で彼女が怒る。
そういう距離で、俺たちふたりは長い旅を続けている。

ふたりで、元気にはしゃぎたい夜もあれば、
ひとりで、静かに酔いたい夜もある。
ふたりで、寄り添っていたい夜もあれば、
ひとりで、冷たい風に吹かれたい夜もある。

同じ空間で過ごす膨大な時間を通して、
「ひとりの自由」ではなく、
「ふたりの自由」を探し始めている。

「結婚」という名の約束で始まった「永い旅」は、
生まれて初めて、「他の人間」というものと、
心底本気で向かい合うチャンスをくれた。

Our Freedom

if I yawn, there's an 80% chance she will too
if I fart, there's a 90% chance she'll be angry
in those distances, the two of us are continuing
this long journey

some nights, we want to have fun together
other nights, I want to have a quiet drink alone
some nights, we snuggle together
and other nights, I want to feel the cold wind alone

through the enormous amount of time spent
in the same space together
I find myself searching not for "freedom of one"
but for "freedom of two"

this "Long Journey" that began with a promise of "marriage"
has given me the first chance in my life to seriously
face "another person" with all of my heart

愛されたいと願うばかりで、愛することを忘れていないか？

Wanting to BE LOVED so much...
have you not forgotten TO love?

性格

大自然で、大都会で、いろんな人々の「性格」に触れる。

人間には、大きく分けると「農耕民族的な人」と「狩猟民族的な人」がいるんだ、って思った。

農耕の世界には「仕事が出来る、出来ない」といったような、せちがらい人物評価基準はない。穏やかに繰り返される、ささやかな楽しい毎日が美徳。狩猟の世界では、それぞれが全体の目標のために役割分担し、その組織を最も有効に動かすためにリーダーが生まれる。こういう世界では、人間の有能無能が問われるし、毎日が勝負の連続で、当然、勝つことが美徳になる。

もちろん、優劣はない。
それぞれに幸せのカタチがある。

そう考えると、今までの超狩猟的なオレは、その人の性格を見ようとせず、農耕的な人を無理矢理に狩猟的な世界に引きずり込み、「デキル、デキナイ」という評価基準にのせ、苦しめていた気がしないでもない。

俺自身は、相変わらず超狩猟的な世界を生き続けていこうと思うが、この旅に出掛けたことで、初めて、農耕的な世界を受け入れる心の幅を持てた自分を感じて、最近、妙に嬉しいんだ。

Personality

In the great outdoors, in big cities, I come across many different "personalities."

If broadly categorizing humans, there are the "Farming Type" and the "Hunting Type."

In the farming world, there is no cheap judgement system of "who can do the job, and who can't do the job". The calm routines and small pleasures of everyday life are virtues.
In the hunting world, roles are assigned in order for the whole to achieve a goal.
The role of a leader is born to manage the group to effectively achieve those goals.
In this world, a person's abilities and competence are challenged, and everyday is a succession of competition. And of course, victory becomes a virtue.

Neither is superior.
Both worlds possess their own types of happiness.

With that in mind, I have no doubt that until now, I lived deep in the hunting world.
And without trying to see personalities, forced the farming type into the hunting world and judged them on the basis of "Can or Can't"; not realizing how much suffering that may have caused.

I will probably, as always, continue to live deep in the hunting world, but because of this journey, I know now I have the heart to accept this farming world for the first time.
Lately, weird...how that makes me happy.

バリ、ウブドゥの夜

そこらに座り込み、ギターを弾いていると、タトゥーだらけの腕にギターを抱えた若いバリニーズがぞろぞろ集まってくる。

車座になり、まずは握手。
オレがオリジナルのラブソングを唄い、彼らはジョン・レノンを唄う。
静まり返ったモンキー・フォレストに俺たちの唄声と蛙の鳴き声だけが響いている。

唄っては語り、語っては飲み、飲んでは唄う。
テーマは決まって女と夢で、手元には缶ビールとタバコが転がっている。

千葉のさびれた地下道で、湾岸ヤンキーと弾き語りをしていたときと、なにも変わらない。
路上の夜は、人を裸にする。

ギター教本など買えず、テープを擦り切れるほど聞いて練習したというNYOMAN。
彼の唄う「JEALOUS GUY」は、史上サイコーに胸に浸みるぜ。

Night in Ubud, Bali

while sitting there, playing my guitar
some young Balinese with guitars and tattooed arms
began gathering around

we gather into a circle, and then handshakes
I sing an original love song, and they sing John Lennon
in the silenced monkey forest
the sound of frogs and our singing voices are
all that could be heard

sing and then talk, talk and then drink,
drink and then sing.
the theme is always "Women" and "Dreams"
with beer cans and smokes at our fingertips
exactly like the times I spent performing in Chiba's
run-down underpass with my bay-area, punk friends
nights out on the road, strip people

Nyoman couldn't afford to buy a guitar textbook
so he practiced by listening to tapes over and over
until they almost wore out
his version of "Jealous Guy" moves my heart
more than any other in history

アジアの片隅で

頼りない地図を片手に小さな村々をバイクでさまよう。
市場の片隅で、路上の屋台で、お祭りの縁日で....
バリニーズの日常に潜り込み、お互いにたどたどしい英語を駆使した世間話に花が咲く。

「アジアの一員として、世界のトップレベルにある日本という国の経済発展を誇りに思う」
「確かに、日本人をマネーマシーンとしか見ない人もいるけど、オレは同じアジアの一員として日本人に特別の親近感があるよ」
「アジアの一員として、NAKATAという日本人がイタリアで活躍してくれているのは、オレにとっても嬉しいんだ」
意外にも、そんな言葉をよく聞く。
特に若い奴らの日本へのオモイは、アツイものがある。
新鮮な驚きだ。

「アジアの一員として....かぁ」
オレは、生まれて初めて、自分が「アジア人」であることを意識した。
「人間はみな本質的には同じ。西洋も東洋もあるか」という気持ちもある反面、
「オレはアジア人である」というフィーリングが、妙に心の奥でピンとくるのは、なぜなんだろう？

In a Far Corner of Asia

with an unreliable map in hand, wandering through
small villages by motorcycle, in a corner of a market,
at a food stand on the road, at a fair during a festival...
creeping into the daily lives of the Balinese
making small talk with each other in broken English

"As a member of Asia, I am proud of Japan's world-leading
economic development."
"Of course, there are some that only see Japanese as
'money machines', but as a member of Asia, I feel a
special closeness to the Japanese."

"As a member of Asia, it also makes me happy to know
that NAKATA, a Japanese, is active in Italy."
Surprisingly, I hear opinions like these quite often
There is something passionate towards Japan,
especially the younger generation
A fresh surprise

"Hmm...as a member of Asia"
For the first time in my life, I am aware that I am "Asian"
On one hand, I feel, "People are essentially the same.
There is no West or East."
But at the same time, why is it there's something that
hits home with this feeling of "I am Asian"?

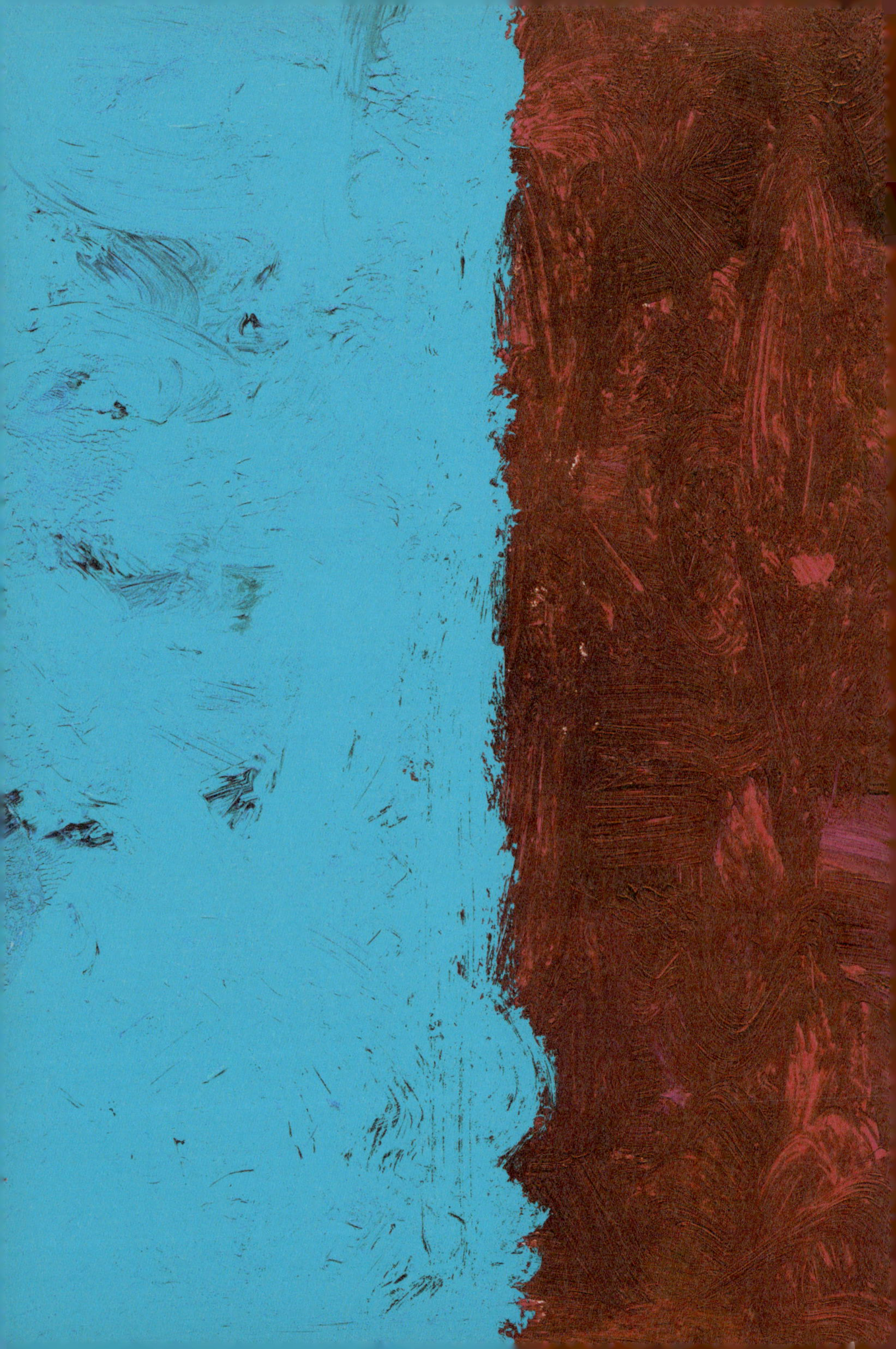

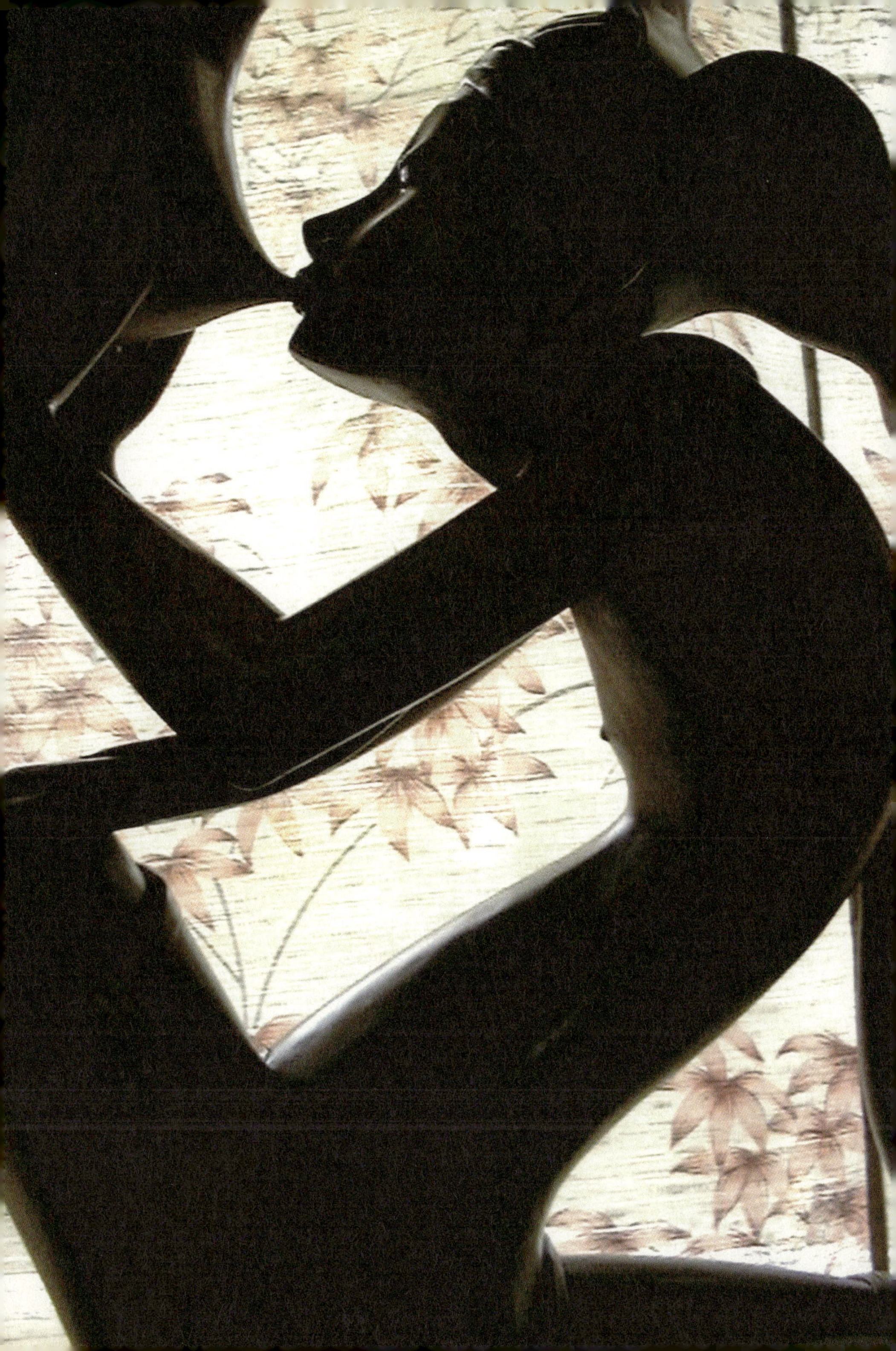

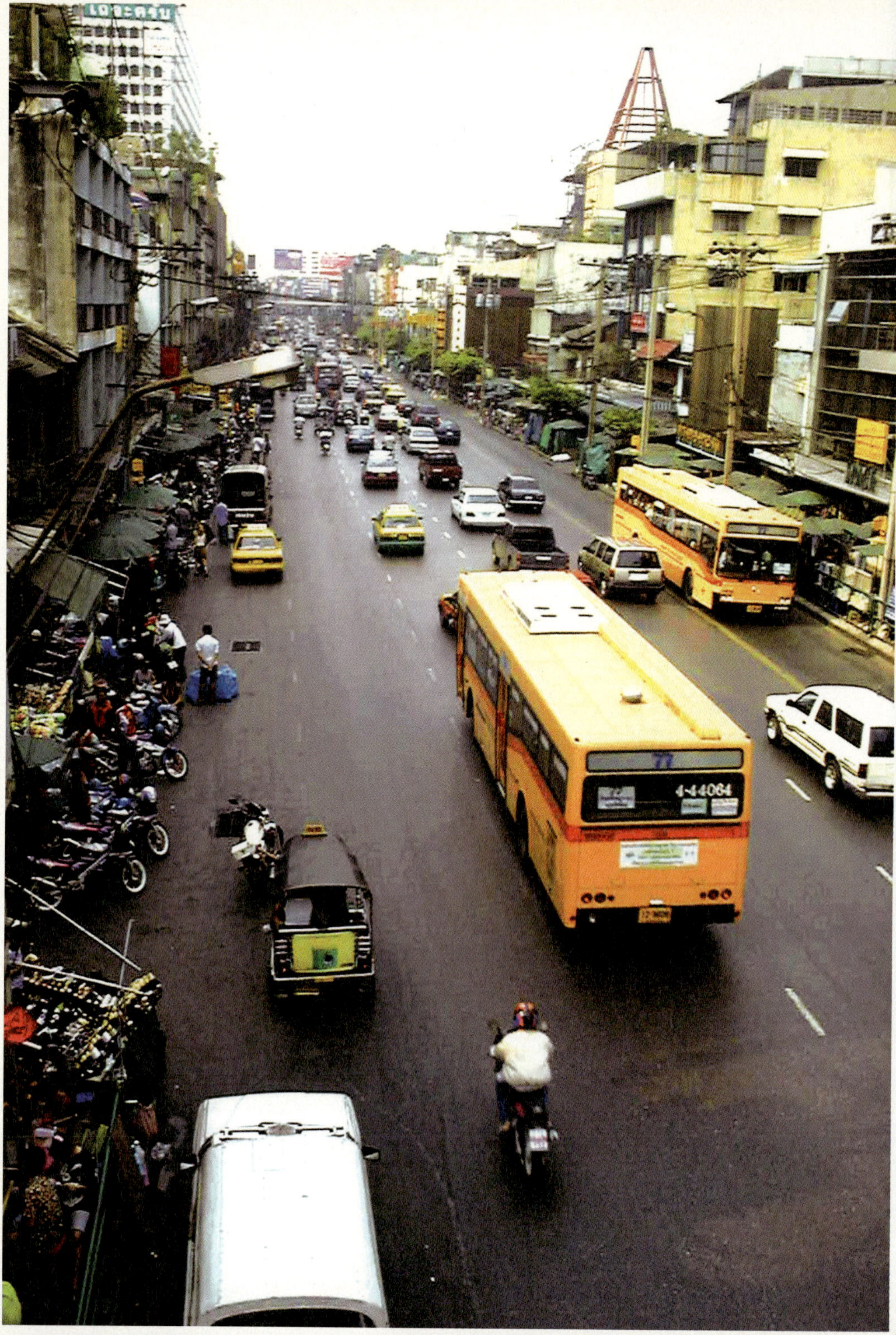
4-44064

Khaosan Road

The crossroad for the world's backpackers: Khaosan Road in Bangkok.
Lined with cafes, cheap hotels, and travel agencies, the streets overflow with suspicious food stands.
Travelers drifting through Asia come to this road, meet, exchange stories, and then continue their travels.

Going to travel agencies on Khaosan Road is fun.
All over, inside,
"I want to go from Kathmandu to New York, stopping off in Delhi."
"Is there a long-distance bus going from Phnom Penh to Saigon?"
"Does a 'Long Neck Tribe' really exist in Chiang Mai?"
"How much is a ticket through Jakarta to Sydney? Could I stop off in Bali?"
Exciting, world-wide conversations are taking place.
I'm feeling the vibe of a familiar face, Mr. Knop, whose favorite line was, "You don't need a guidebook. You don't need a plan either. An Asian trip is just to come to Khaosan Road and then decide where you want to go."

カオサン・ロードにて

世界中のバックパッカー達のクロスロード、バンコクのカオサン・ロード。
安宿とカフェと旅行代理店が並び、道には怪しい屋台が溢れている。
アジアを漂う旅人達は、この通りで出逢い、物語を交換し、また旅立っていく。

カオサン・ロードの旅行代理店に行くと、楽しい。
そこら中で
「カトマンドゥからデリーに寄ってニューヨークへ帰りたいんだ」
「プノンペンからサイゴンへの長距離バスってある？」
「チェンマイには、ホントに首長族いるんですか？」
「ジャカルタ経由でシドニーへのチケットはいくらですか？バリにも寄れますか？」
なんて、ワクワクするようなワールドワイドな会話が飛び交ってる。
顔なじみになったノップさんの口癖どおり、
「ガイドブックなんていらねぇ。プランもいらねぇ。アジアの旅なんていうのは、
カオサン・ロードに来てから、どこ行くか決めりゃいいんだよ」ってノリ。

なんかこの通りの雰囲気が好きで、屋台の脇に座ってタバコを吹かしていると、
いろんな奴が気軽に話しかけてくる。
「日本人？」
「うん。アンタは？」
「オレ？イギリス。アレックスっていうんだ」
「オレ、アユム。よろしく」（握手）
「アユーム、どのくらい旅してんの？」
「今、4ヶ月くらいかな」
「結構長いねぇ。なんか目的みたいなもんあるの？」
「いや〜、別に。せっかく地球に生まれたんだし、面白いところ全部見ないと
もったいねぇなぁ〜と思ってさ」
「賛成！」
「アレックスは、どんなルートで旅してんの？．．．」
そんな調子で、たあいもない会話が始まる。

それにしても、ラリった瞳でボケーっとしてる奴の多いこと、多いこと。
マリファナ色に染まる旅人たちのクロスロードでは、
いろんな意味で、ヘブンズ・ドアーが君を待ってるぜ。

I like the atmosphere on this road. Sitting along side
a food stand, smoking a cigarette, all kinds of people
come up and start talking to me.
"Japanese?"
"Yeah. You?"
"Me? British. I'm Alex."
"Hi, I'm Ayumu." (handshake)
"Ayumu, how long have you been traveling?"
"About 4 months?"
"That's pretty long. You got some kind of purpose?"
"No. I want to see and feel all around world.
I was born on Earth, so...all interesting places,
I want to see."
"Cool!!"
"Alex, where did you go?"
Just like that, a conversation starts.

Still, there are so many...so many, vegged-out people
with eyes that are stoned.
At the crossroads of travelers dying themselves in
the color of marijuana,
Heaven's door is there waiting for you, in various ways.

LIFEWORK

100以上の島々が浮かぶタイ・パンガー湾。
晴れ渡る青空の下、ボートで静かな海を漂い、いくつかの島に上陸を繰り返す楽しい小冒険。

一緒にボートに乗ったカーネルサンダース風おじさんは、よっこらしょっとオレの隣に腰掛け、突然、質問を発した。

「アンタのライフワークはなんだい？」

名前でも、年齢でも、国籍でも、職業でもなく、このおじさんは「ライフワーク」を一番最初に聴いた。

ライフワーク....
自分の一生をかけて追いかけるテーマ。
好きな方法で、好きなペースで、大好きなことを自分なりに究めていく作業。
もちろんテーマは、ペットの研究から宇宙の神秘、四十八手まで、大小問わず何でもあり。

「正直言って、ライフワークなんて考えたことなかったなぁ。まぁ、今考えると....
オレのライフワークは....『強くて優しくてビッグな男の研究』ってとこかなぁ」

オレの答えに、カーネルはうんうんとうなずいて微笑するだけだった。
(やべぇ、もっと具体的に言った方がよかったかなぁ) なんて思ったりもしたが、
オレも彼に聴いてみた。

「アナタのライフワークは、なんですか？」

そしたらカーネルはひとこと、
「HUMAN BEING」だって。

オイオイ、オレより漠然としてんじゃねぇかよ、こら！

LIFEWORK

Phang Nga Bay, Thailand, where over a 100 islands float
under a sunny blue sky, flowing across the quiet sea by boat
landing on various islands, enjoying small adventures

A Colonel Sanders-like man slowly sat down next to me
on the boat, and out of the blue, popped a question.

"What's your lifework?"

not my name, age, nationality, or occupation
this man first asked about my "lifework"

LIFEWORK...
a theme one spends a lifetime chasing
mastering a work through any method you like
at any pace you like
on whatever you love
of course, the theme can be anything
from "pets" to "the mysteries of space" to
"48 sexual positions"
doesn't matter how big or small

"Honestly, I've never thought about my lifework.
Well, if I think now...my lifework is...
'I want to be a strong, kind, and BIG-hearted man.'
...or something."

The Colonel just nodded and grinned at my answer.
I thought to myself, "Oh crap. Maybe I should have
explained in more detail...", and asked him the same question.

"What's your lifework?"

And the Colonel answered, "HUMAN BEING."

Hey, hey...that's even a fuzzier answer than mine!! Come on!

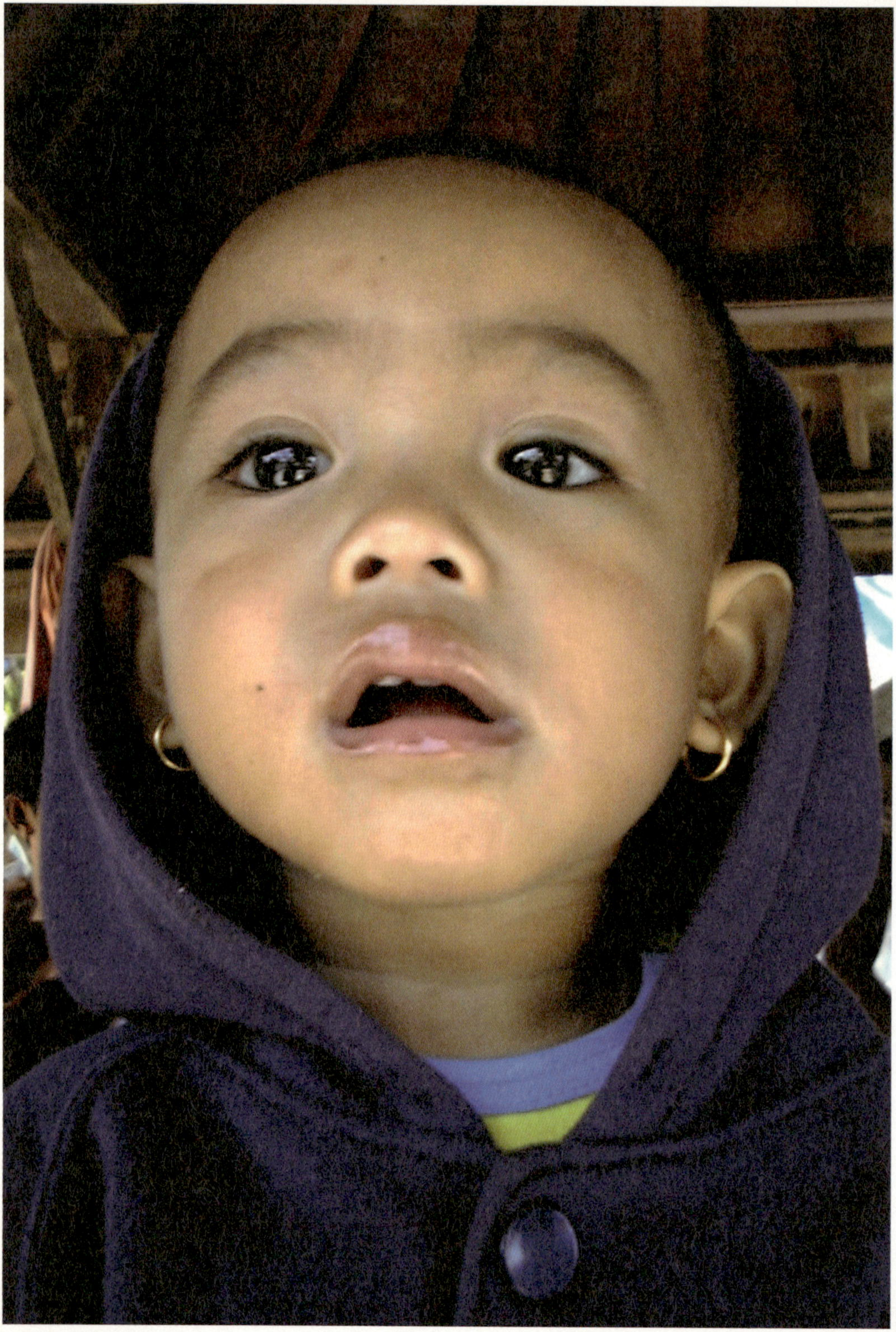

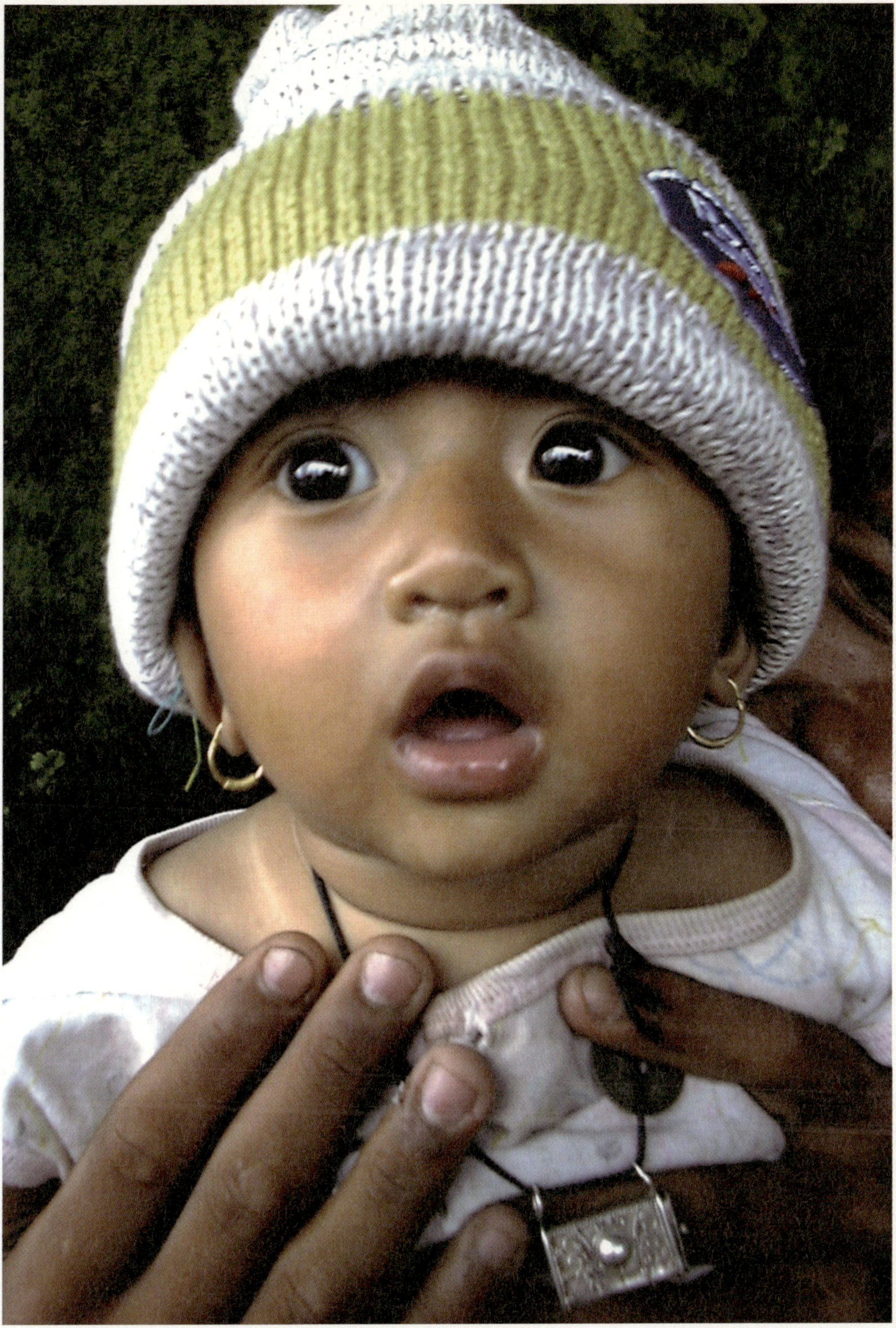

あるヒッピーの語った
「LIFE OF SOME ISLAND 〜ある島の一生」

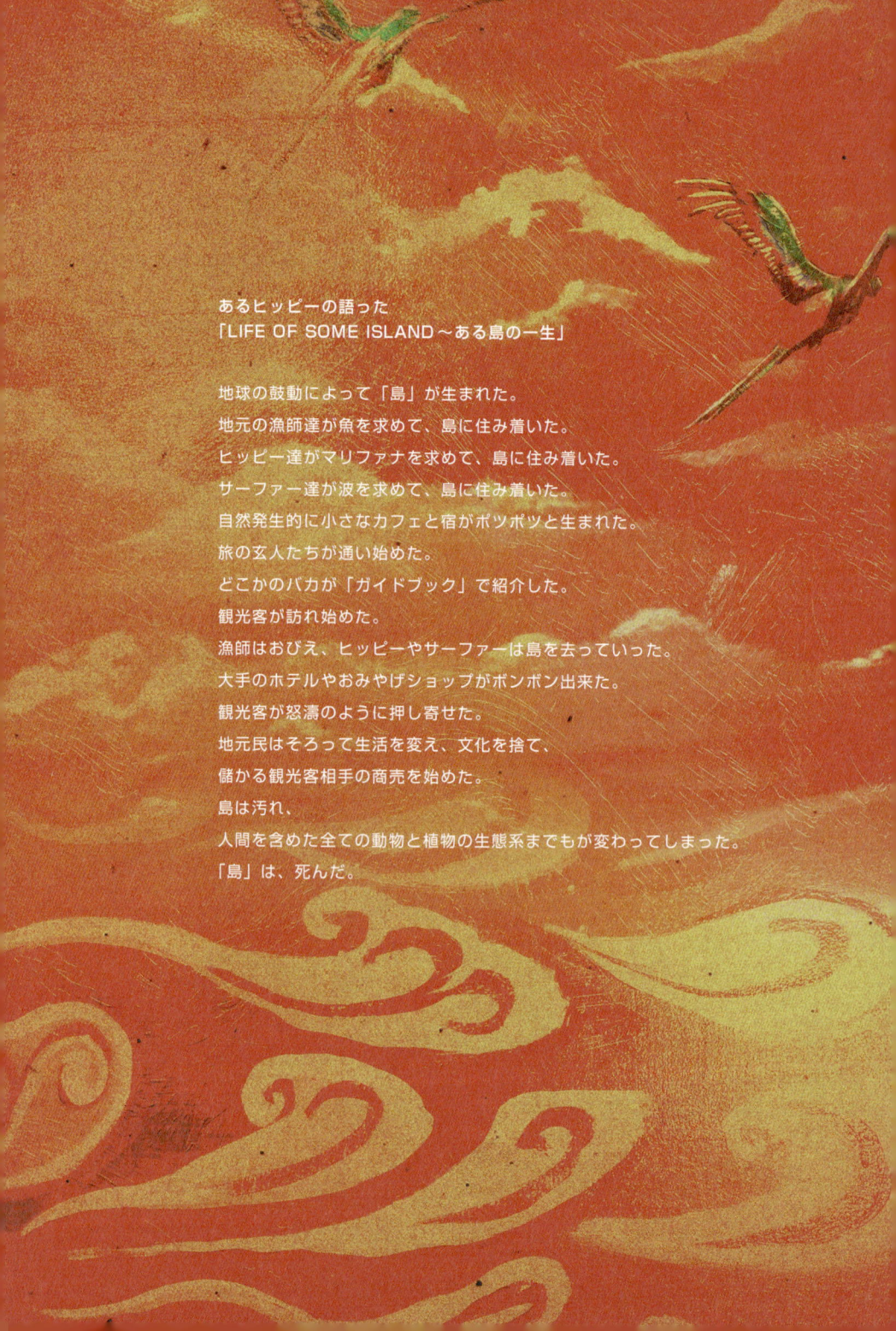

地球の鼓動によって「島」が生まれた。
地元の漁師達が魚を求めて、島に住み着いた。
ヒッピー達がマリファナを求めて、島に住み着いた。
サーファー達が波を求めて、島に住み着いた。
自然発生的に小さなカフェと宿がポツポツと生まれた。
旅の玄人たちが通い始めた。
どこかのバカが「ガイドブック」で紹介した。
観光客が訪れ始めた。
漁師はおびえ、ヒッピーやサーファーは島を去っていった。
大手のホテルやおみやげショップがポンポン出来た。
観光客が怒濤のように押し寄せた。
地元民はそろって生活を変え、文化を捨て、
儲かる観光客相手の商売を始めた。
島は汚れ、
人間を含めた全ての動物と植物の生態系までもが変わってしまった。
「島」は、死んだ。

"Life of Some Island" - Told by some Hippie

the Earth's pulse brought an "island" to life
local fishermen, in search of fish, settled on the island
hippies, in search of marijuana, settled on the island
surfers, in search of waves, settled on the island
small cafes and inns spontaneously began to appear
here and there
expert travelers started coming
some idiot introduced the island to a "guide book"
tourists started visiting
fishermen got scared, hippies and surfers left the island
big name hotels and gift shops began to pop up all over
tourists plowed in
all the locals changed their lifestyles
threw away their culture
and started profitable tourist businesses
the island got polluted
the lives of all plants and animals, including the people,
had changed
the "island" died

おれとおまえのほにゃらら

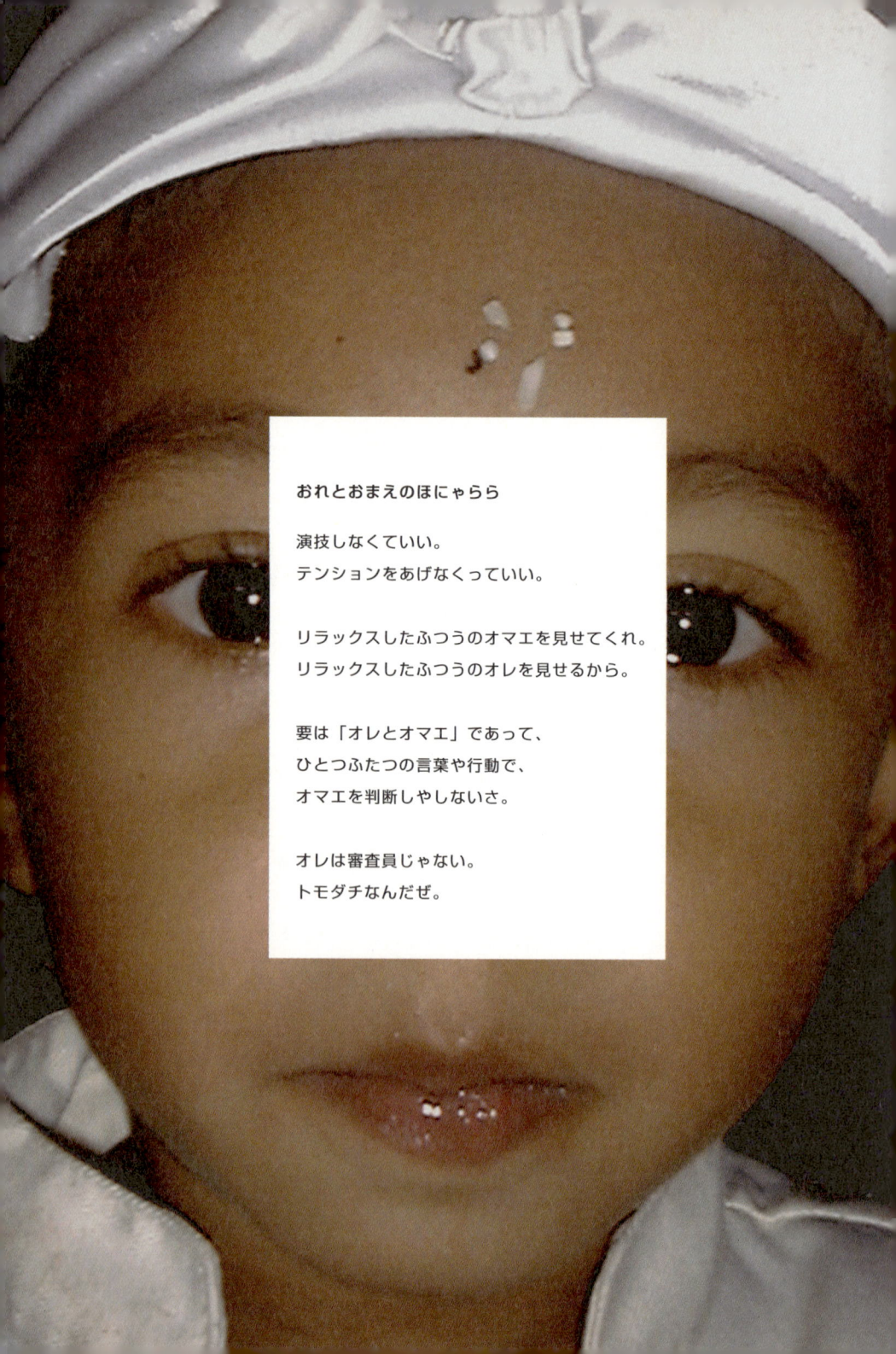

演技しなくていい。
テンションをあげなくっていい。

リラックスしたふつうのオマエを見せてくれ。
リラックスしたふつうのオレを見せるから。

要は「オレとオマエ」であって、
ひとつふたつの言葉や行動で、
オマエを判断しやしないさ。

オレは審査員じゃない。
トモダチなんだぜ。

You and Me...

no need to pretend
no need to get worked up

show me the usual, relaxed You
I'll show you the usual, relaxed Me

the important thing is "You and Me"
a few words or something you did
I won't use them to judge you

I am not a judge
I am your friend

でっかい花

ゆっくりやりてぇなら、胸張ってゆっくりやろうぜ。
ぶらぶらしたけりゃ、飽きるまでぶらぶらしようぜ。
ココロに引っかかることがあるなら、納得できるまで遠回りしようぜ。
「年相応の世間体」なんて気にしてたら、自分を小さくするばかり。
「人生」とは、生まれてから死ぬまでの全ての期間をさすんだ。

「人生、男子は一事を成せば足る」
いつか、死んじまう日がくる前に、
一回でもいい、一瞬でもいい、
命を精一杯輝かせた、
でっかい花、咲かそうな。

Huge Flower

if you want to go slowly, let's go slowly
with our heads held high
if you want to just hang, let's hang until we're bored
if something bothers you, let's take a detour
until you're satisfied
if you pay too much attention to "acceptable appearances"
you'll lose yourself
"life" points to the entire period of time
between birth and death

"in life, a man is worthy if he achieves for one instant"
one day, before your time is up
just once is enough, for one moment
let's make our life shine with all our might
and make that huge flower bloom

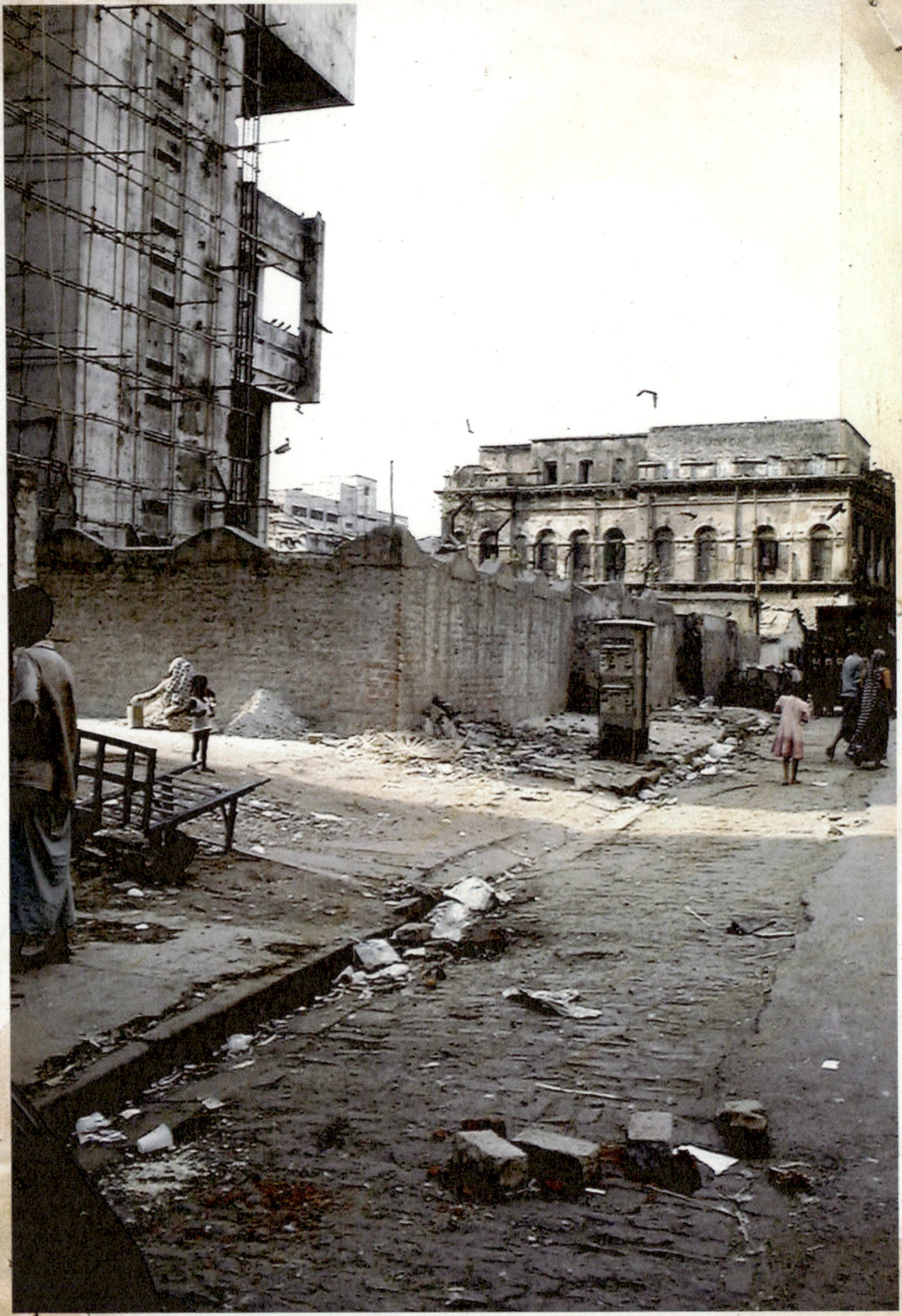

In the Calcutta - Prologue

Standing in the streets of Calcutta, India,
there is nothing I can do.

I walk past an old lady, thinning from starvation,
laying face-down on the muddy ground;
not knowing if she is dead or alive.
I walk past a child, as thin as a twig,
clinging to the old lady's leg.
I walk past a man, lost in a pile of trash,
with flies swarming infected flesh wounds.
I walk past children, crawling the ground with their
remaining limbs, desperately trying to cling to me
with their small hands.
Showered with the sound of car horns and angry voices
yelling, "Japanese! Money! Money! Please!", I just
look up at the sun setting in the exhaust fumed sky
of Calcutta.

The "make-dreams-come-true ME" I should have obtained
in that space called TOKYO, couldn't do anything.
The "eloquent ME" I should have obtained in that
space called TOKYO, couldn't do anything.
The "ME" I should have obtained in that space called TOKYO,
was unexpectedly powerless.

"I hope, at the very least, this pain I feel will change me..."
My whole heart said to me.
At that moment, I thought,
"Anything. Right now, righ there, I will do something."

In the Calcutta - Prologue

インド・カルカッタの路上に立ち、オレはなにもできない。

生きているのか、死んでいるのかもわからない様子で、泥だらけの地面にうつぶせに倒れているやせ細ったおばあちゃんの横を通り過ぎる。
倒れているおばあちゃんの足にしがみついている枝のような赤ちゃんの横を通り過ぎる。
ゴミの中に埋もれ、傷ついた皮膚が膿み、そこにハエがたかっているおじさんの横を通り過ぎる。
残された片方の足で地面をはいずり回り、小さな手でオレの足にしがみつこうとする子供達の横を通り過ぎる。
溢れかえるクラクションと「ジャパニーズ！マネー！マネー！プリーズ！」という怒声を浴びながら、排気ガスまみれの空を見上げるだけの、カルカッタの夕暮れ。

TOKYOという空間で手に入れてきたはずの「夢を叶える自分」は、
なにもできなかった。
TOKYOという空間で手に入れてきたはずの「雄弁な自分」は、
なにも言えなかった。
TOKYOという空間で手に入れてきたはずの「自分」は、
意外に無力だった。

「せめて、この胸の痛みが、新しいオレの誕生であって欲しい.....」
精一杯のココロが、そうつぶやいたとき、
（なんでもいい。いま、ここから、なにかをしよう）と思った。

路上に座り、勇気を奮い、「なにか手伝いましょうか」って、
ひとことだけ、倒れているおばあちゃんに声を掛けてみた。
オレの魂をかけた、不気味な必死のスマイルで。

そしたら、意外にも、おばあちゃんは、無言でニコっと笑ってくれた。
なんだかよくわからないけど、嬉しかったぁ....
一瞬だったけど、初めて、なにかが「交換」された気がしたんだ。

ジョン・レノンの「IMAGINE」が、たまらなく聴きたい夜、
オレはちょっぴりだけど確実に、変わり始めた自分を感じている。

～「優しさ」の反対は、「無関心」である～　　　マザー・テレサ

I sat down in the street, next to an old lady lying there,
and stirred up the courage to say just one phrase,
"Is there anything I can help you with?"
With all my soul. And with an eerie, desperate smile.

Then, to my surprise, she didn't say a word.
She just smiled back.
I don't know why, but that made me happy...
Just for an instant, for the first time,
I felt like we "exchanged" something there.

Unbearably wanting to hear John Lennon's "IMAGINE" that night,
Slowly but surely, I feel the beginning of a change in me.

"The opposite of love is indifference." - Mother Theresa

IN THE CALCUTTA***EPILOGUE

カーリーガート（「死を待つ人の家」）・シシュババン（「孤児の家」）に行き、
故マザーテレサ達の活動を手伝ってみた。

路上に倒れて死にかけていたおじいちゃん達と一緒に、シャワーを浴びた。
手足のひん曲がったおじいちゃん達と一緒に地面にねっころがり、パンを食べた
り食べさせたり。
うんちやしょんべんもたくさんついちゃったけど、なぜか嫌じゃなかった。

触れてみて、壁が崩れた。

オレは、遠くから眺めるだけの偽善者の如く、感傷的になりすぎていた自分が
恥ずかしくなった。
オレは今まで、偏ったイメージによって創られた分厚いフィルターを何枚も通し
て「路上の人たち」と「インド」っていう国を見ていた。

現実は、そんなにブルーじゃなかった。
ほとんどの路上の人にとっては、路上での睡眠が「ライフスタイル」であり、
倒れているんじゃなく、ましてや、死んでいるわけもなく、
ただ、昼寝をしているんだってことを知った。

実際に寝てみるとわかるけど、地面で寝るのは冷たくて意外と気持ちいい。
それに、本人達は、決して悲しんでいるばかりじゃない。
みんな思ったより明るくて、思ったより楽しんでて、思ったよりギャグで、
思ったよりイージーだった。

言うまでもなく、もちろん深刻な面は多々あるが、それだけで見ると感傷的にな
るだけで、リアルは見えてこない。
何となくオレの目から過剰なフィルターが溶け始め、
「なにか」がクリアーになった。

In the Calcutta - Epilogue

Went to Kalighat (house for the dying) and Shishu
Bhavan (orphanage) to help with the work of the
late Mother Theresa.

I showered with old men dying in the streets.
I lie on the ground with old men with twisted arms
and legs, feeding them bread and eating with them.
I got lots of urine and feces on me, but for some
reason, it didn't bother me.

I touched, and a wall collapsed.

Like a hypocrite just watching from afar, I was
embarrassed to be overly sentimental.
Until now, I've seen "street people" and "India"
through thick, unbalanced filters due to biased images.

In reality, it wasn't that blue.
Most of those people I saw lying in the streets,
I found out that it was part of their lifestyle.
Not sick, not dying, but merely napping.

You'll understand if you actually try it. Lie down
and the ground is cool; unexpectedly, it feels
quite nice.
And; they aren't exactly all sad.
Everyone was happier than I imagined, enjoying
themselves more than I imagined, were funnier than
I imagined, and more easy-going than I imagined.

Needless to say, of course there are many serious
situations, but only seeing those parts would just
make you sentimental, and be blind to reality.
Somehow, those extra filters began to melt away
from my eyes, and "something" became clear.

そこには、悲しみや痛みではなく、
数千年の歴史によって創られた「現実」と、「これから」があるだけだった。

「お互いに、がんばろうね！オレも今日から、オレに出来そうなこと、
探してみるからよ！」

近いうちに、カルカッタの夕暮れをもう一度見たいと思った。

There, it was not sadness or pain,
There existed just the REALITY of thousands of years
of history, and the FUTURE.

"Let us both do our best. I'll start looking today
to find something I can do!"

I thought to myself, I'd like to see the sunset in
Calcutta again soon.

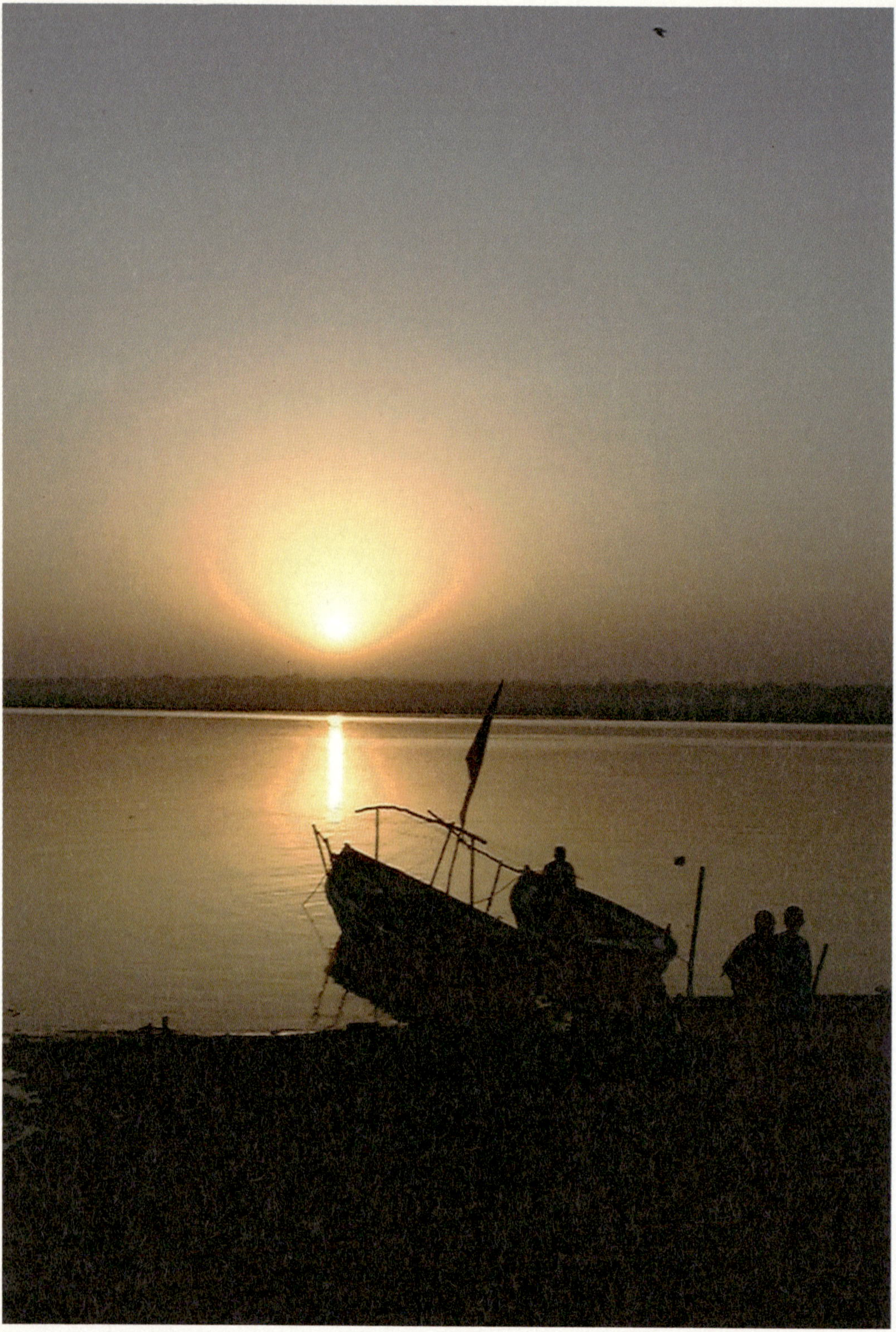

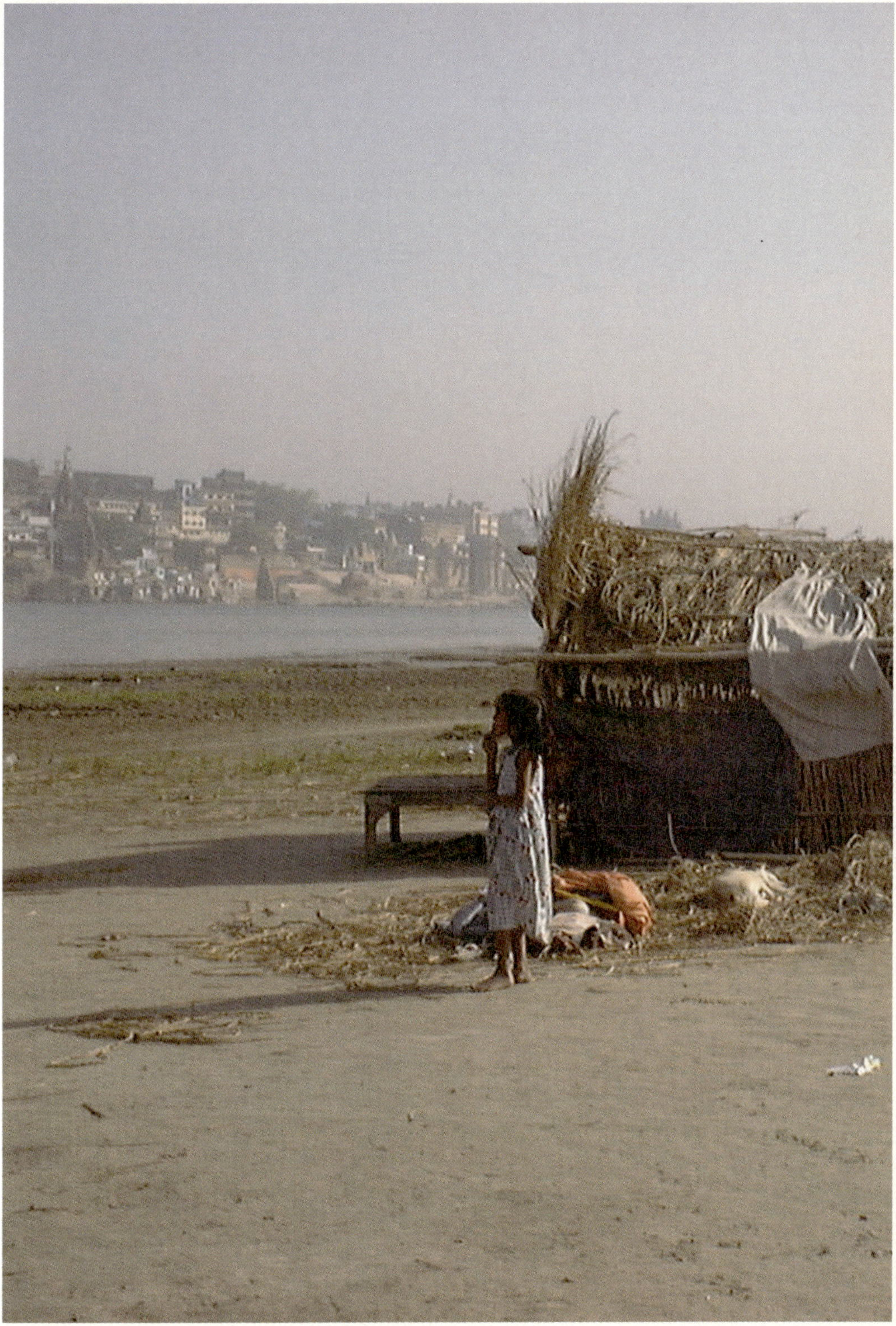

something beautiful　〜なにか美しいもの〜

シシュバパン（「孤児の家」）では、オレもサヤカもピンク色のエプロンをかけて、
大忙しだ。

親に捨てられ、手足が不自由でも、この子たちは極上の笑顔を見せてくれる。
1枚しかもらえなかったクッキーを半分に割って、
オレにくれる優しさを持っている。
人間のぬくもりに飢え果て、がむしゃらにオレの胸に顔を押しつけてくる子供た
ちの全身から、マッスグナチカラが伝わってくる。

こいつらは、MONEYにではなく、FOODにでもなく、
LOVEに飢えているんだ....

そんな子供たちを胸に抱きながら、顔を上げてふっと我にかえると、
急に涙が溢れそうになってしまうのは、なぜなんだろう。

Something Beautiful

In Shishu Bhavan (orphanage), Sayaka and I both wear
pink aprons, and become busy bodies.

Whether they were abandoned by their parents, or
physically disabled, these kids will flash their
biggest smiles.
Even with the one cookie they are given, they have
the kindness to give me half.
Starving for human warmth, they recklessly press
their faces into my chest.
And from their entire body, I sense a straightforward
energy.

These little guys; starving not of MONEY, not of FOOD,
but of LOVE...

Holding these kids in my arms,
I look up and back at myself,
Why is it, all of sudden, tears are about to overflow?

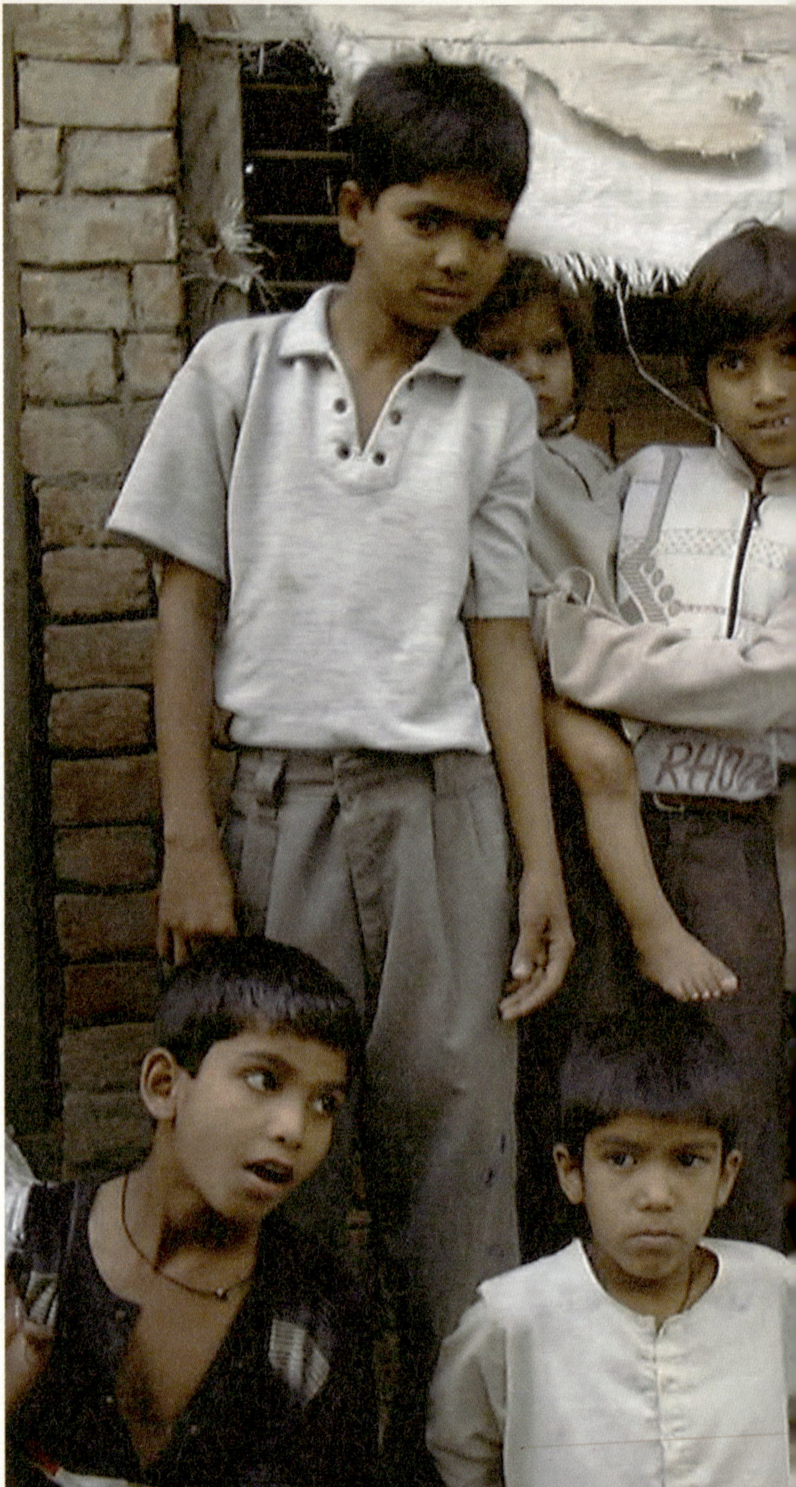

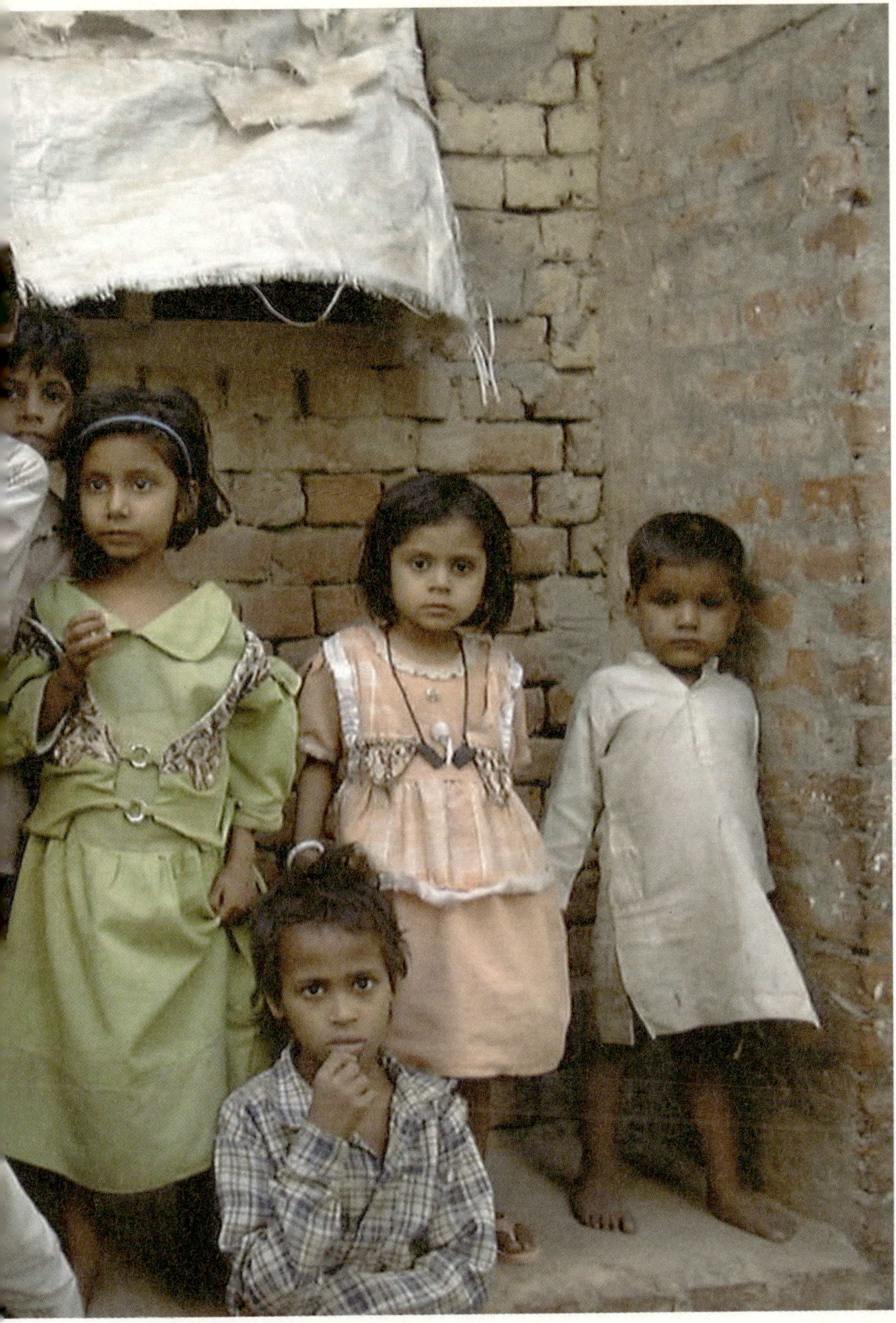

デジカメ

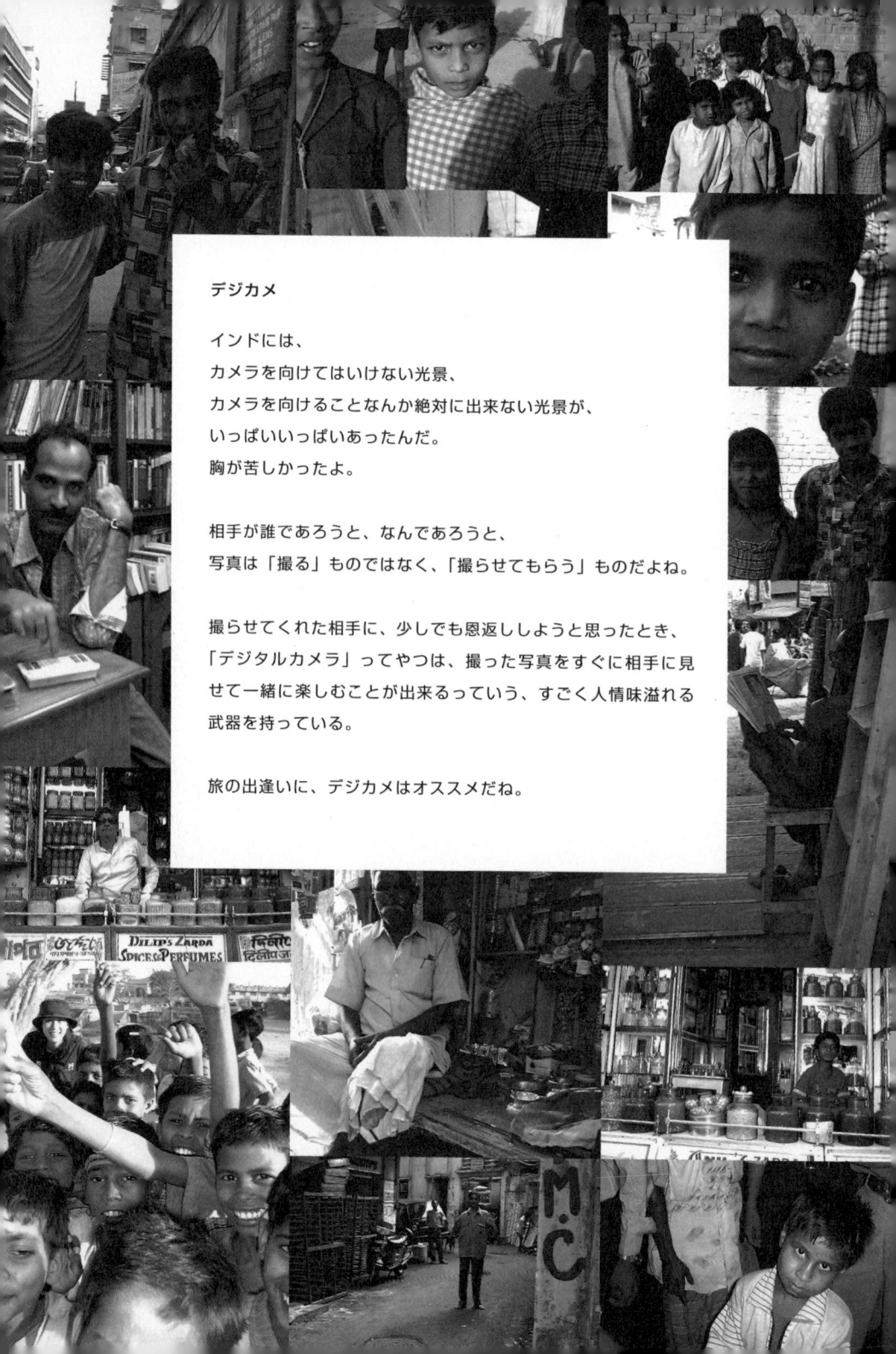

インドには、
カメラを向けてはいけない光景、
カメラを向けることなんか絶対に出来ない光景が、
いっぱいいっぱいあったんだ。
胸が苦しかったよ。

相手が誰であろうと、なんであろうと、
写真は「撮る」ものではなく、「撮らせてもらう」ものだよね。

撮らせてくれた相手に、少しでも恩返ししようと思ったとき、
「デジタルカメラ」ってやつは、撮った写真をすぐに相手に見せて一緒に楽しむことが出来るっていう、すごく人情味溢れる武器を持っている。

旅の出逢いに、デジカメはオススメだね。

Digital Camera

in India
a scene the camera should not focus on
a scene the camera could never focus on
there are tons and tons of
my heart ached

Whoever it may be, whatever it may be,
Photos are not things to be "taken",
but should be things they "let you take", right?

For a person that lets me take their picture,
if I wanted to return the favor just a little,
the digital camera lets you show them that
picture right away and can be enjoyed together.
I carry with me this great heartwarming tool
to repay kindness.

For encounters on a journey, I recommend the
digital camera.

ちゃれんじとれいん

<PART: 1>
近くにスラム街が広がり、観光客への盗難や強盗が多発するという悪名高いカルカッタ・ハウラー駅で電車を待つ。
「かなり観光客はカモにしてきましたよ」系のオーラを出した悪人面の人々。
ホームのはずれにしゃがみ込んでいる俺たちの周りを、囲むように歩き、ちらちらっと隙をうかがっている。
真っ暗だし、荷物重いし、サヤカもいるし、なんかあっても逃げられねぇなぁ、やべぇ....
(ココでビビってちゃ、男がすたる!パート1!)と思って、平然を装いながらギターをポロンポロンならして、T-BOLANの「離したくはない」を熱唱。

オォー!意外にこの曲はインド人マインドにヒットしたらしい。

急にニコニコして「GOOD!GOOD!ONE MORE!」だって。
なんだいい人達じゃん。
でも、ギターって便利だ。

Challenge Train

Part 1:
Surrounded by the slums, where tourists are often victims of theft and robbery,
We wait for a train at the notorious Howrah Station in Calcutta.
There are some people with bad auras about them that says, "We've made suckers of many tourists."
We sit down on the far side of the platform,
they walk around as if to surround us,
And they peek for any slight chances.
It's pitch dark and...our packs are heavy and...
Sayaka is with me and...If something happens,
we can't get away. Ahhh, shit...
(If I chicken out here, my manhood is on the line! Part 1!), I thought to myself...
I coolly began strumming my guitar and sang
T-BOLAN's "Don't Wanna Let You Go" with all my heart.

Wow!! Surprisingly, this song was a hit to the Indians!

Suddenly, smiling they said, "Good! Good! One more!"
Hey, these guys aren't so bad after all.
Anyway, the guitar comes in handy.

<PART: 2>
無事に列車に乗り込み、寝台車の喫煙所でタバコを吹かす。
「かなり実戦くぐってますよ」系のオーラを出したカーキ色の制服を着た軍人たち。
一秒で1000発くらい弾が出そうなライフルを持って、オレを囲むように座り始める。
5人だから一秒5000発で、オレのアタマはスイカみたいにコナゴナ....
(ココでビビってちゃ、男がすたる！パート2！) と思って、平然を装いながら
「タバコ吸う？」なんて言ったら、
急にニコニコして、「THANK YOU」だって。
なんだ、いい人達じゃん。
でも、タバコって便利だ。

Part 2:
Safely boarded the train, having a cigarette in the smoking area of the sleeping carriage.
There are military guys wearing khaki colored clothing with an aura about them that says, "We've been through a few battles."
With rifles that look as if they could fire 1000 bullets per second, they sit around as if to surround me.
Five of them, that's 5000 bullets per second.
My head could be shot to mash potatoes...
(If I chicken out here, my manhood is on the line! Part 2!!)...I thought to myself,
I coolly said, "Smoke?" and offered a cigarette.
Suddenly, smiling, he said "Thank you."
Hey, these guys aren't so bad after all.
Anyway, cigarettes come in handy.

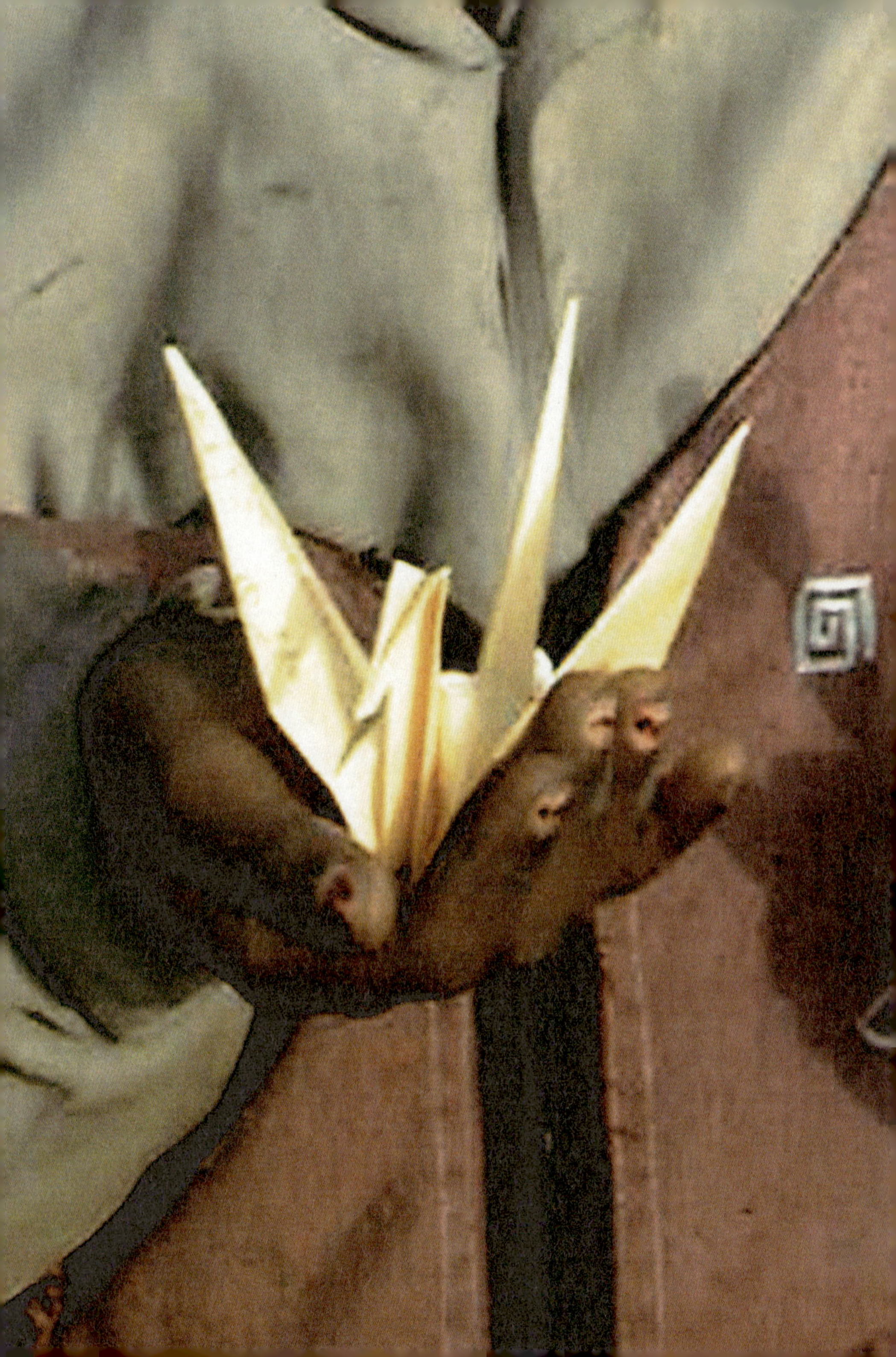

Crane

"wanting to give something that is Japanese,
and doesn't cost any money"

the Origami Cranes that Sayaka folded
hope they continue to live in the hearts of
the children around the world...

鶴

「日本を感じることが出来て、お金の掛からない贈り物をしたいね」

サヤカが折った「折り紙の鶴」が、
世界中の子供たちの胸に棲み続けてくれますように....

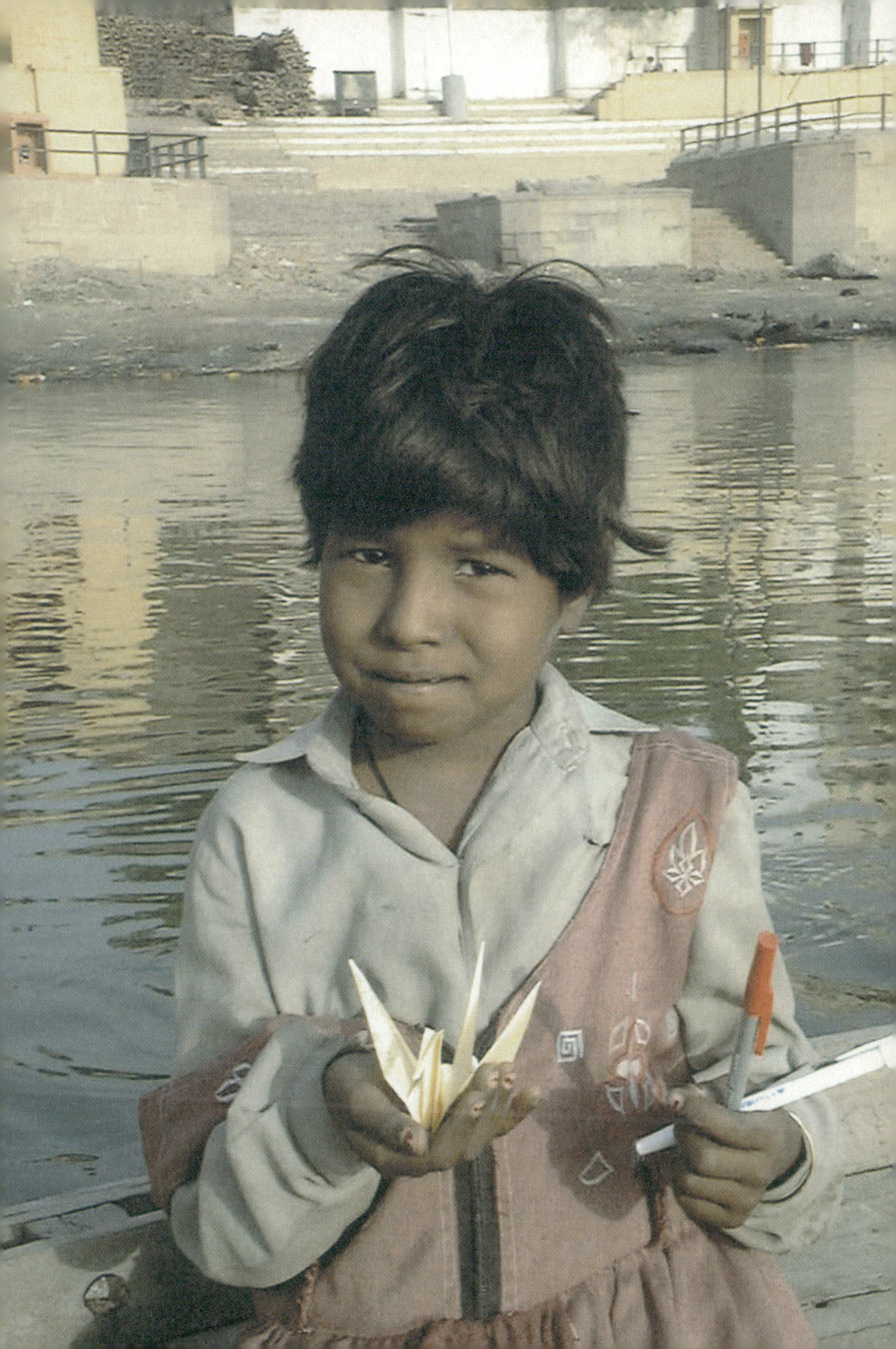

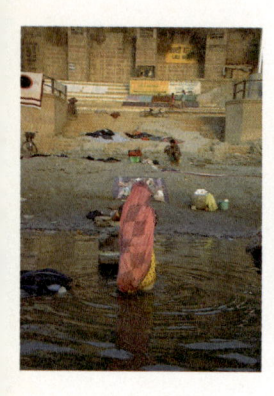

人生の持ち時間

ガンジスから贈られるさまざまな心象は、オレに、
「自分の人生の持ち時間」ってやつを意識させる。

日常の流れの中では忘れてしまいがちだが、人生は無限じゃない。
「人生の持ち時間」は、限られている。
誰にとっても、「終わり」へのカウントダウンは確実に始まっている。

まだまだやってみたいことも、逢ってみたい人も、行ってみたい場所も、見てみたいものも、食べてみたいものも、知りたいことも....いっぱいいっぱいある。
そして、「自分の生まれてきた目的」を知り、成し遂げなければ、という使命感もある。

このままじゃ終われないぜ。
やったる！

Life's Time Limit

various impressions presented to me from the Ganges River,
I become conscious of "my life's time limit".

there's a tendency to forget through the flow of
daily life, but life is not forever.
life's time is limited
for anyone, the countdown to the end has surely begun

but still, there is so much I want to try, people I
want to meet, places I want to go, things I want to see,
food I want to eat, things I want to know...
there is so, so much
and then, to know "the reason why I was born"
and I have a sense of duty to complete my mission

I can't finish like this.
I'll do it!

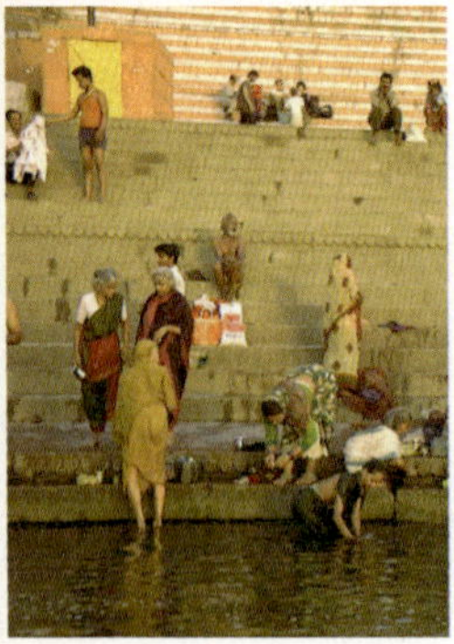
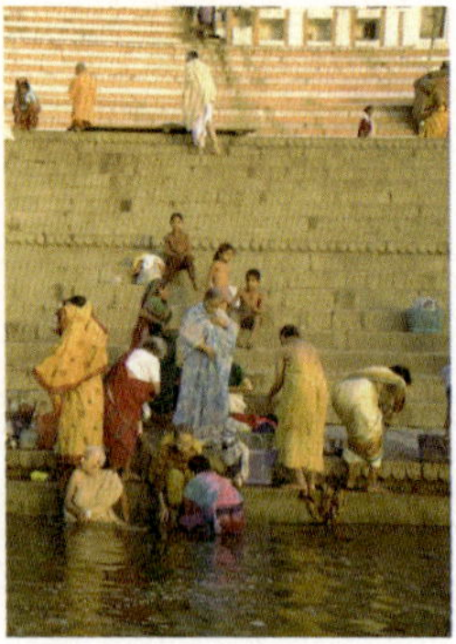

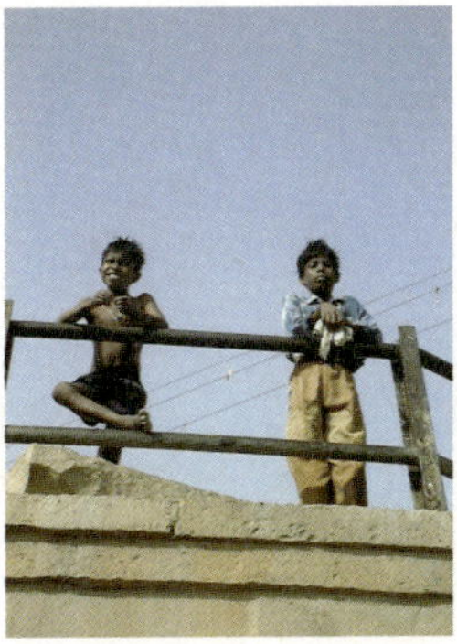
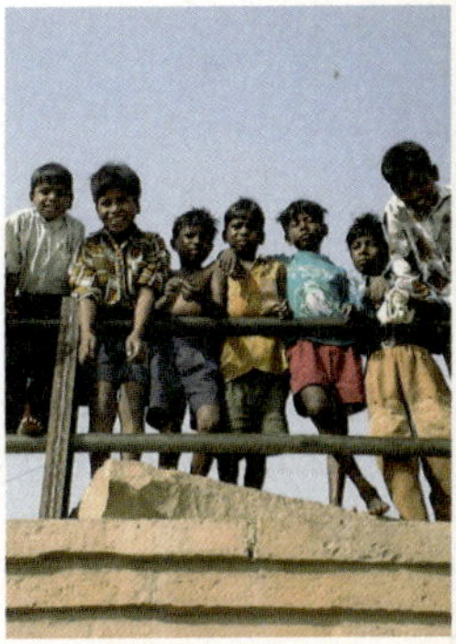

ノミにも負けず

ノミにも負けず、シラミにも負けず、
あの手この手で近寄ってくるフレンドリーな悪人達にも負けず、
40度を超えるハンパじゃない暑さにアタマはボケ、
無造作に鳴り続けるクラクションに耳は麻痺し、
白く濁る排気ガスだらけの空気にのどはやられ、
果物の腐ったようなニオイに鼻はひんまがり、
物乞いの手をかいくぐり、押し売りの手をかいくぐり、
それでもふたり、大きなバックパックを背負い、手を取りながら、
神出鬼没魑魅魍魎百花繚乱の9億人の人種のるつぼの中を、
トコトコトコトコ歩き続ける。

インド人って優しいとか、一風変わった体験ができたとか、
そんな軽いものじゃなく、
イイもワルイも都会も田舎も全部ひっくるめて、
とにかく「濃い」の一言に尽きる国。

短い間だったけど、インドを夫婦で旅するのは、
「旅行」というより、「修行」でした。

お台場での爽やかなデートが、ちょっぴり懐かしいです。

Not Defeated by Fleas

not defeated by fleas, not defeated by lice
not defeated by the friendly hands of criminals that approach here and there
brain-dead from the crazy heat, well past 40 degrees
ears paralyzed by the continuous, unsettling sounds of traffic horns
throat done in by the cloudy, white, exhaust-fume infested air
nose about numb from the smell of rotten fruit
slipping through the hands of beggars, slipping through the hands of peddlers
and still the two of us, with huge packs on our backs, holding hands
through the melting pot of 900 million people
all types of unbelievably good and evil
we walk, and walk, and continue to walk

Indian people are gentle; I was able to have unusual experiences...
it's not that easy to describe.
the good and bad, city and countryside, all of it together
at any rate, this country is simply, in one word, **"DEEP"**

it was a short time, but traveling as a couple
through India was more a "training" than a "trip"

Those refreshing dates back in Odaiba (Tokyo)
I miss them just a bit

ストリートチルドレン

世界中の街角で出逢う、痩せこけてぎょろぎょろした瞳をしたガキンチョ達。
左手でおなかをさすりながら、右手をオレに向かって差し出し、
「HUNGRY...MONEY...FOOD....」と泣きそうな声でささやく彼ら。

そんな哀しい瞳で見つめられるたび、オレは意味不明な罪悪感にかられながら小銭をあげたりあげなかったりしていたが、今日、ちょっとした発見をした。
たまたまヒマだったオレは、路上で右手を差し出してきたガキの横に並んで座り、一緒にコーラを飲み、彼の似顔絵を描いてプレゼントしてあげたんだ。
ノートの切れはしに描いた超へたくそな似顔絵なのに、ガキンチョは歓声を上げて大喜びしてくれた。
そのとき浮かべた笑顔は、お金をあげたときの笑顔とは比べモノにならないほど、かわいかったんだ。
ほんっと、いい顔してた。

飢えたガキンチョだけじゃなく、オレも同じだ。
お金はもちろん欲しいけど、
「誰かと優しく向き合って過ごす時間」っていうのが、いちばん欲しいのかもし

Street Children

on the street corners around the world, I meet kids
thinning away with goggling eyes
rubbing their bellies with their left hand, holding
out their right hand to me
on the verge of tears and whispering
"HUNGRY...MONEY...FOOD..."
every time they stared with those pitiful eyes
I would be overwhelmed with an incomprehensible sense
of guilt, giving them change sometimes
but today, I made a small discovery
just happened to have time to spare
I sat down next to a kid that held out his right hand to me
drank a coke together
and drew a portrait and gave it to him as a gift
it was a really sucky drawing on the corner of a piece
of notebook paper
but the kid shouted out with joy
that smile was the cutest
the smiles I got when I gave them money couldn't compare
really, a beautiful face

not just starving children, but me too
of course we want money
"spending affectionate time with someone" is maybe
what we really want the most

この海が好きだから....

「この海が好きだから、オレはこの海を守りたいんだ。ただ、それだけだよ」
「昔から海を探検するのが大好きだったんだ。だからこの仕事をしてる。昔からの夢が叶ったってわけさ」
「美しいものが壊されていくのを見てると哀しくなるんだ。だからオレは戦ってる」
「高度なテクノロジーの溢れる都会の暮らしもいいけど、
オレはシンプルなテクノロジーときれいな海があれば毎日サイコーの気分だよ」

スールー海で出逢ったフィリピンの海を守る男達。
毎日毎日、大好きな海に潜り、マジメに遊んでる奴らだ。
今まで「環境問題」ってものを語る人達にはいっぱい逢ったけど、
こんなにかっこよくて気持ちいい奴らは初めてだった。

彼らの生き方やコトバはシンプルだったけど、
優しくて、強かった。
そして、めちゃくちゃHAPPYだった。

歩く道は、それぞれ違うけど、
同じ年齢の同じ男として、オレも負けてらんねぇな。

Because I Love this Ocean...

"Because I love this ocean, I want to protect it.
That's all."
"I've always loved exploring the ocean. That's why
I chose this job. So this is a dream come true."
"It's sad to see something beautiful destroyed.
That's why I continue to fight."
"A life in a city overflowing with high technology
is alright, but simple technology and the beautiful
ocean are all I need to enjoy everyday to its fullest."

A group of guys I met at Sulu Sea, protecting the
oceans of the Philippines.
Each and every day, they dive into the ocean they love,
and seriously enjoy life.
I've met a lot of people that talk about
"environmental issues",
But I've never met anyone as cool and pleasant as
these guys.

their lifestyles and words were simple,
but were kind and strong.
and, were so very HAPPY.

The paths we take may differ,
But as a man of the same age, I'll do my best too!

おれは、いま、ここにいる

知識ではなく実感を。
バーチャルではなくリアルを。
明日ではなく今を。
主張ではなく愛を。
世間ではなくアナタを。

すべては、ひとつ。
ココロの根を伝う。

オレの人生。
たった一度の人生。
燃焼する命。
溢れ出す生命力。
魂のフォーカス。
シンプルなパワフル。
魂のライン。
天のサイン。

おれは　いま　ここにいる。
オレハ　イマ　アイシテル。

I - right now - am right here

Not knowledge, but feelings
Not virtual, but real
Not tomorrow, but now
Not assertion, but love
Not the public, but you

All is one
Along the roots of the heart

My life
Only one life
A burning life
Overflowing power to live
Focus of soul
A simple powerfulness
Line of soul
Sign of heaven

I - right now - am right here
I - right now - love

Journey 3 :

Eur

asia

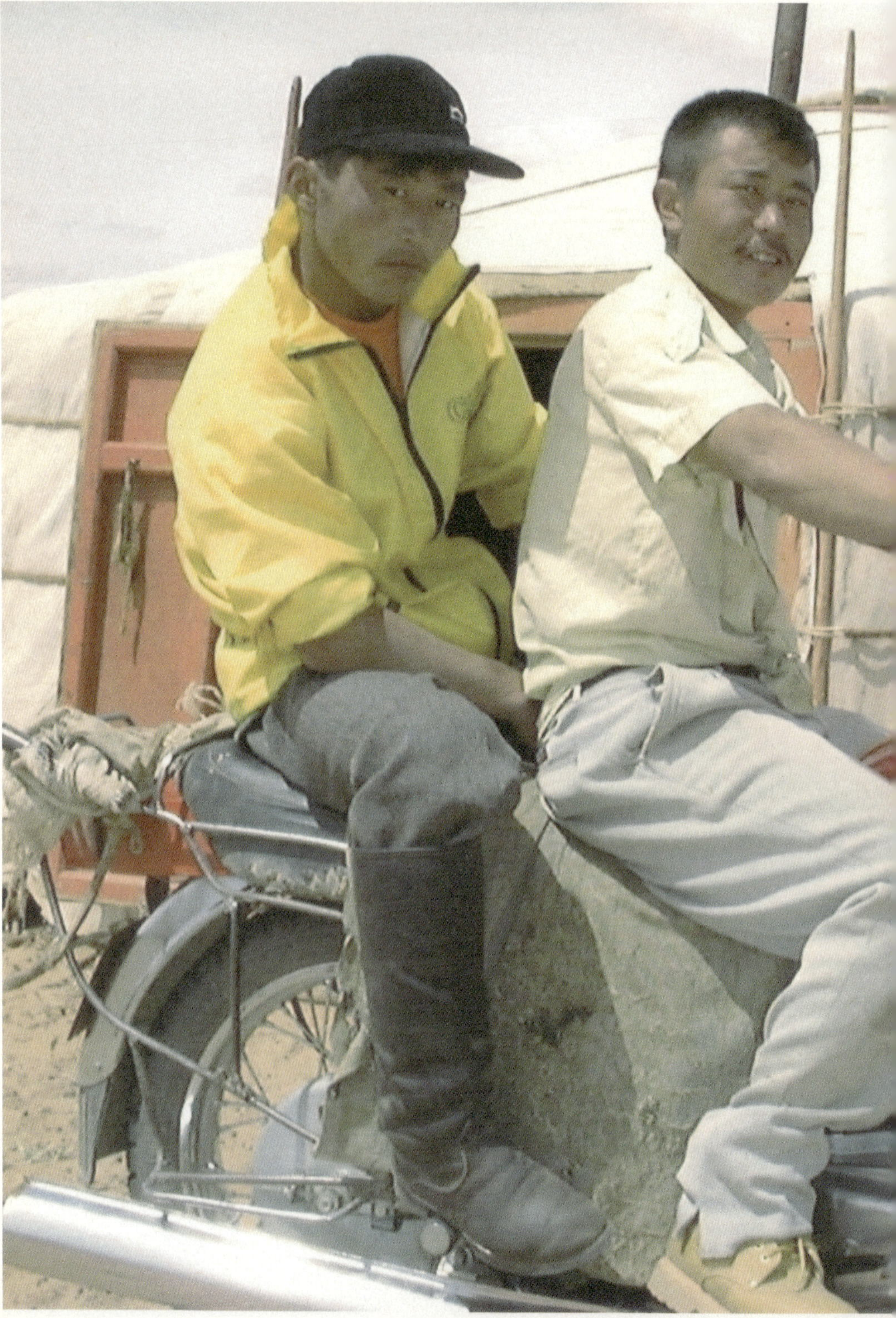

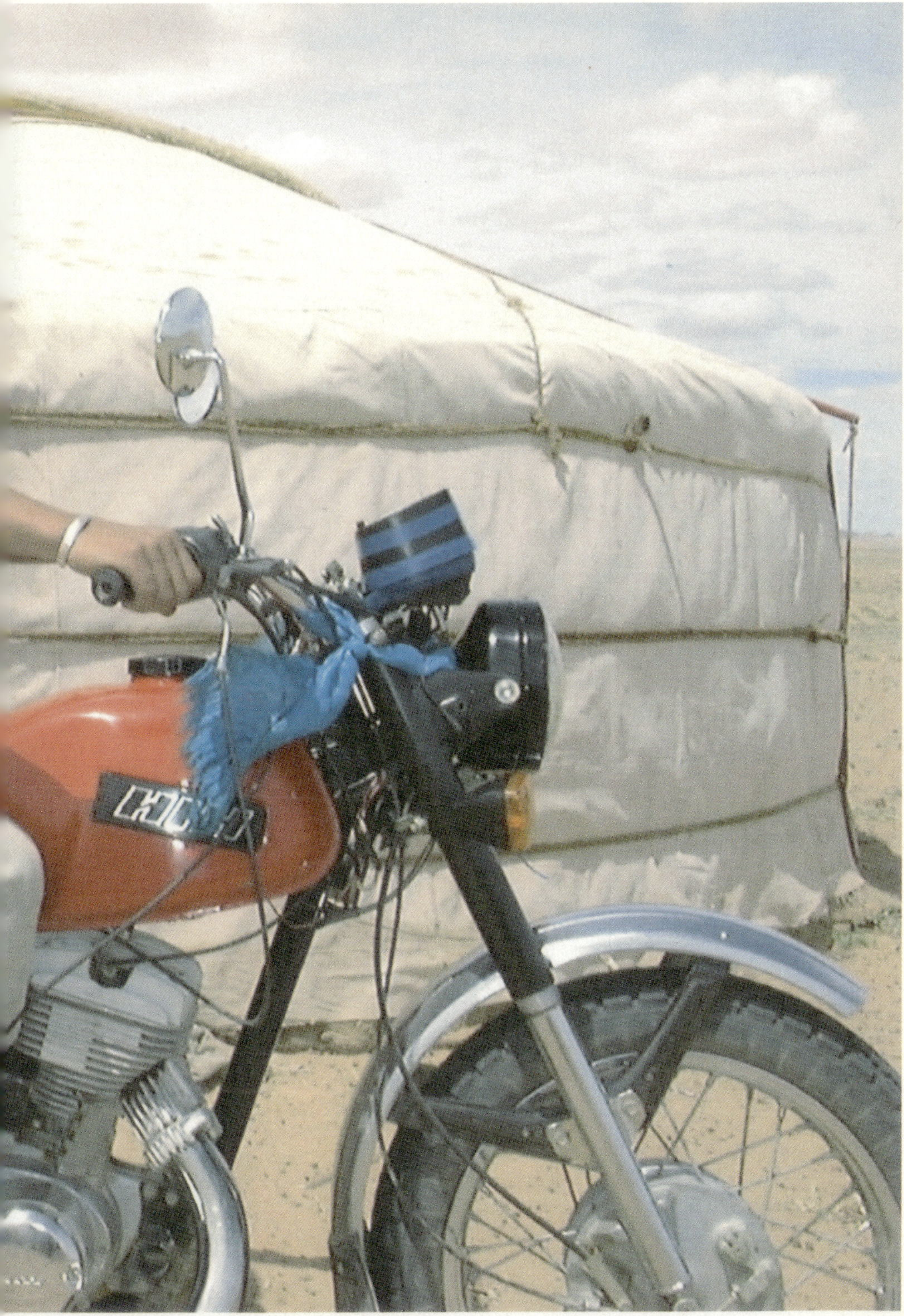

大草原

サヤカとふたり、モンゴルの大草原に立つ。

青い空、白い雲、蜃気楼、そして360度の地平線。
なにもない。誰もいない。

ふたりが、無限に広がっていくような感覚。
ふたりぼっちで、ポツンとここに存在しているというリアル。

「自分の女さえ幸せに出来ない奴に、日本も地球も幸せに出来ない」

そんな想いが、心を吹き抜けていく。

Great Grass Plains

Sayaka and I both, stand in the great plains of Mongolia.

Blue sky, white clouds, a mirage, and a 360 degree horizon.
There is nothing. There is no one.

The two of us, spreading out infinitely.
Just the two of us, the reality of our existence alone
here out in the middle of nowhere.

"A guy who can't make his own woman happy, can't
possibly make Japan or the Earth happy."

That thought, passes through my heart at that moment.

えっ？ほんとに？ココで暮らすの？

「サァ〜、いよいよ、モンゴルかぁ。遊牧民になっちゃうぜ！」なんて、
気軽な気持ちで出掛けていった、モンゴル大草原での遊牧民ライフ。
待っていたのは、「観光客扱い一切ナシの現役バリバリ遊牧民ファミリーとの
ディープな暮らし」だった。

トイレは大小ともに草原だし、
ゲル（遊牧テント）のまわりは家畜達のクソまみれでハエがわんさかいるし、
ゲルの中はかなりほこりっぽくてノミみたいな虫が飛んでるし、
メシは山羊ミルクご飯（コレは食えない）とカレー的炒め物（コレは食える）
だけみたいだし、
部屋の明かりはろうそくのみだし、
冷たい飲み物は一切ないし、
シャワーなんて夢のまた夢だし、
水は細菌がウヨウヨした水をちょっと使えるだけらしい....
さらに、ファミリーのみんなとは、言葉がまったく通じない。
やっぱ甘くねぇ。
都会っ子のカップルには、遊牧民ライフは強烈だぁ。

まぁ、オレは大丈夫だろうけど、サヤカがいつまでもつか....
まさか、サヤカに野グソをさせることになるとは....

そんな心配をしながら、大草原の真ん中にポツンとたたずむゲルの中、
初日の夜の毛布にくるまっているオレ。
ぐーがぁーぐーがぁーぐぐぐぅがぁー
このファミリーの主、アグアンサンおじいちゃんのいびきが、ちょっとうるさい
です。

What? Really? Live here?

"FINALLY, so we're here in Mongolia. Let's become nomads!"
we thought casually and headed out to the great plains
of Mongolian nomadic life.
What awaited us was "a really deep lifestyle with
a real-life nomadic family that has never dealt with
tourists before."

The toilet, for both big and small, is the plains.
The area around the GEL (nomadic tent) is surrounded by
fly-infested feces of domestic animals.
Inside the GEL is very dusty and full of flea-like bugs
hopping around.
Food consists only of mountain goat milk rice (not edible)
and curry-like stir-fry (edible).
Candles are the only source of light inside.
Nothing cold to drink.
And a shower...a dream within a dream.
The only water to use is just a little bit of bacteria
infested water.
And on top of all that, we can't communicate with the
family at all.
We underestimated the situation!
Nomadic life for a couple from the city is intense.

Well, I'll be OK, but how long can Sayaka take this...
I never thought I'd make Sayaka take a shit in the
great outdoors...

Worrying about such things, inside the GEL that stands
out in the middle of the great plains, I wrap myself
into a blanket on the very first night.
Guuuu...Gaaaaa...Guuu...Gaaa...Gugugugaaaa...
The head of this family, Aguansan's snoring is just
a bit too loud.

オマエハ　ナニガ　ホシインダ？
それに答えられない人は、旅を続けられないぜ。

WHAT DO YOU WANT?
if you can not answer that,
you can not continue your travels.

満天の星空と野グソの伝説

大草原のど真ん中にひとり、満天の星空に抱かれてする野グソ。
この開放感は、この世のものとは思えない。
もうこのまま死んでもイイや....って思っちゃうくらい、完全にイッちゃってる。

東京ドームをひとりで貸し切って、照明を全部消して、ピッチャーマウンドで
野グソをぶっ放す....
それでも、全然かなわないね。

〜世界で最高の開放感とは、満天の星空の下で野グソをすること、である〜
誰かが言ってた「満天の星空と野グソの伝説」は、やっぱりホントかもしれない。

Legend of a Starlit Sky and Shitting in the Great Outdoors

Alone, out in the middle of the great plains, shitting
in the great outdoors embraced by a starlit sky.
This feeling of freedom is out of this world.
It's almost enough to make me completely believe
"I could die right now and be happy."

Rent the whole Tokyo Dome, turn out all the lights,
and shit on the pitcher's mound...
Even that couldn't beat this feeling.

"The world's highest form of freedom is to shit in
the great outdoors under a starlit sky."
"The legend of a Starlit Sky and Shitting in the
Great Outdoors", that someone once told, may very
well be true.

風

オレとサヤカとバテルテン（遊牧民の男の子）。
３人で羊を追いながら、草原をどこまでも歩いてた。
オレはハーモニカでディランの「風に吹かれて」を吹いてた。

いたずら坊主っぽい笑顔で、バテルテンがオレの手からハーモニカを奪った。
「オマエが吹くのか？」って聞くと、彼は首を横に振った。
そして、彼はハーモニカを風にかざした。
ふぁ〜〜〜ん、ふぁ〜〜ん、ひゅふぁ〜〜ん〜〜〜

風がハーモニカを吹いていた。

強く弱く、細かいビブラートを懸けながら、風は絶妙なトーンでハーモニカを吹いた。
人間の口では絶対に出せない音....
10の音を同時に鳴らした音....

１分ほど、風の演奏を聴くと、バテルテンはニコッと笑って、オレにハーモニカを返した。
「風の音も、サイコーだよね」って？

まいったぜ。

Wind

Bateruten (a nomadic boy), Sayaka, and me.
As the three of us rounded sheep, we walked the
plains endlessly.
I played Bob Dylan's "Blowin' in the Wind" on
the harmonica.

With a grin of a mischievous brat, Bateruten
grabbed the harmonica out of my hand.
"Are you going to play?" I asked, and he shook his head.
Then, held it up to the wind.
Fua---n, fua---n, hyufua---n---

The wind played the harmonica.

Firmly and lightly, applying the slightest vibrations,
the wind played the harmonica with an exquisite tone.
A sound that could never be played by a human mouth...
Ten notes played at once...

After listening to the wind play for about one minute,
Bateruten handed the harmonica back to me, smiling.
As if to say, "The sound of the wind is great too."

Umm...great.

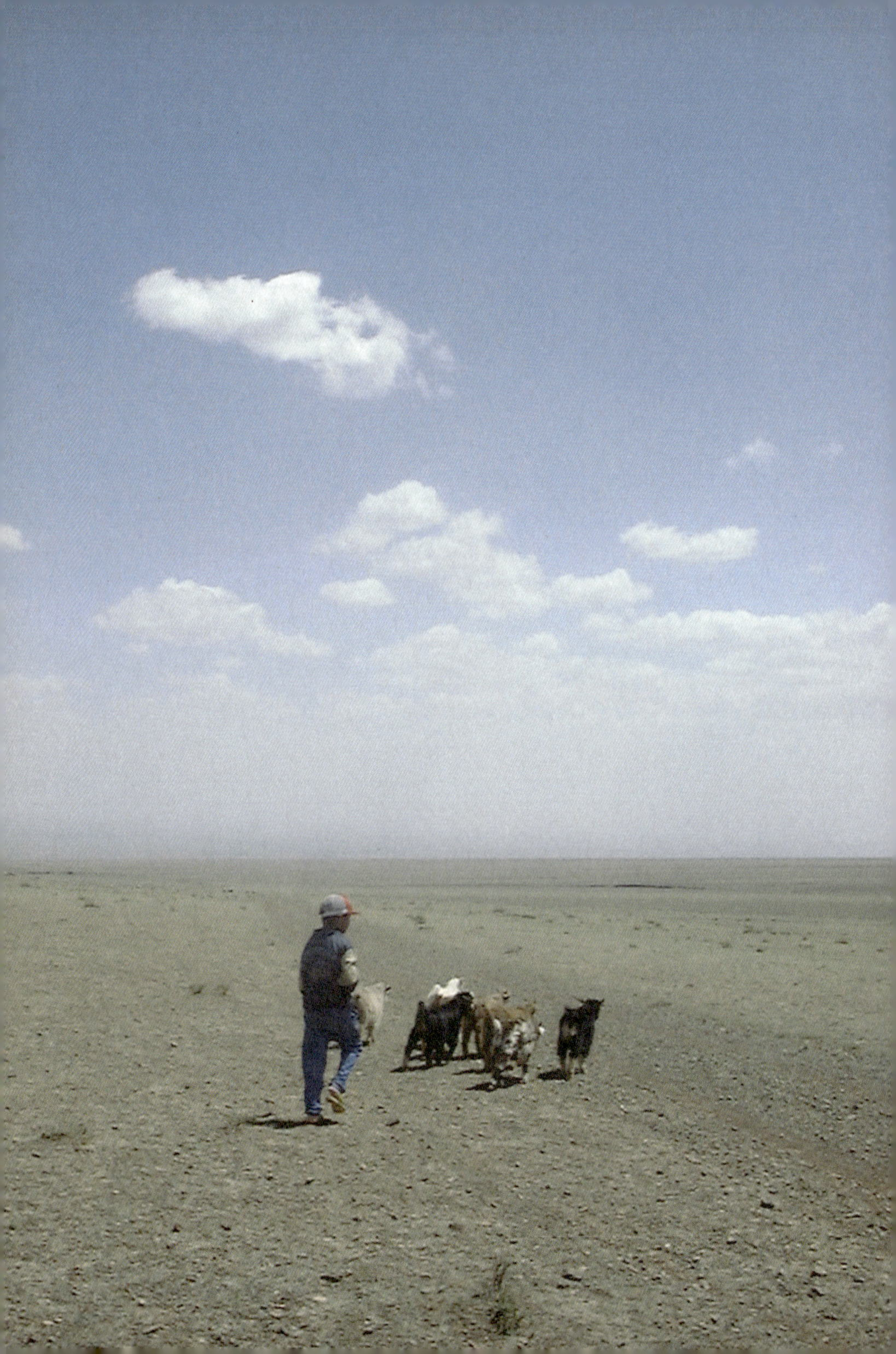

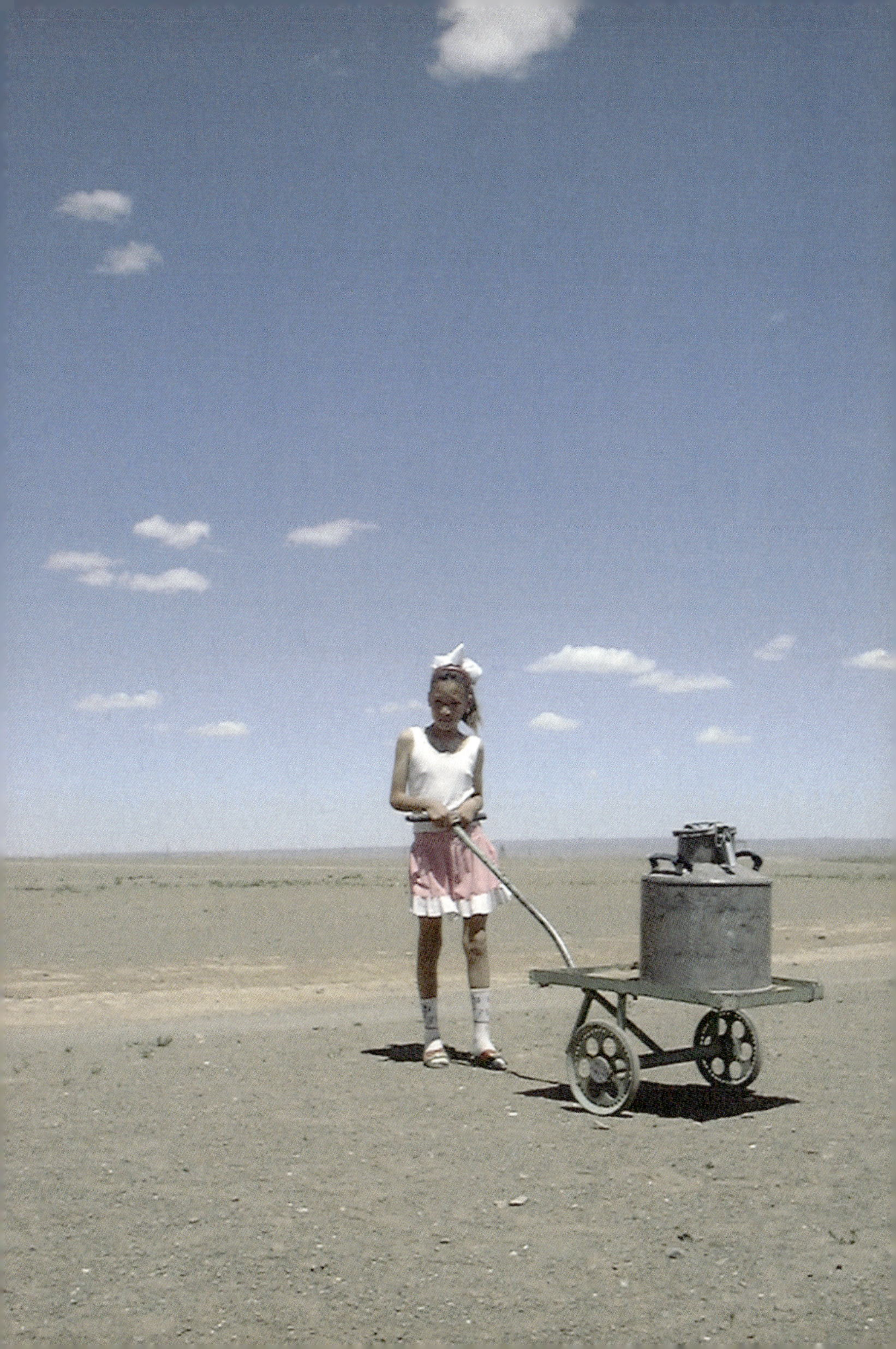

星の音

大草原の夜。
耳をすます。
風が止む。

「完全に音がない時間」を体験したのは、生まれて初めてかもしれない。

完全な静寂に入った途端、理由もなく、急に怖くなった。
しばらく我慢して、落ち着いてくると、満天の星が、
しゃらしゃらしゃらしゃら....
って小さく鳴っていることに気づいた。

へぇ〜。
星にも、音があるらしい。

Sound of the Stars

the great plains at night
I listen carefully
the wind stops

"a time with absolutely no sound"
for the first time ever, I experienced this

in that instant of absolute silence
for no reason at all, suddenly I was afraid
I was patient for a while, started to calm down
then the stars of the full sky are...
Shala, shala, shala, shala...
are ringing ever so slightly, I noticed

hmm...
apparently, stars have sounds too

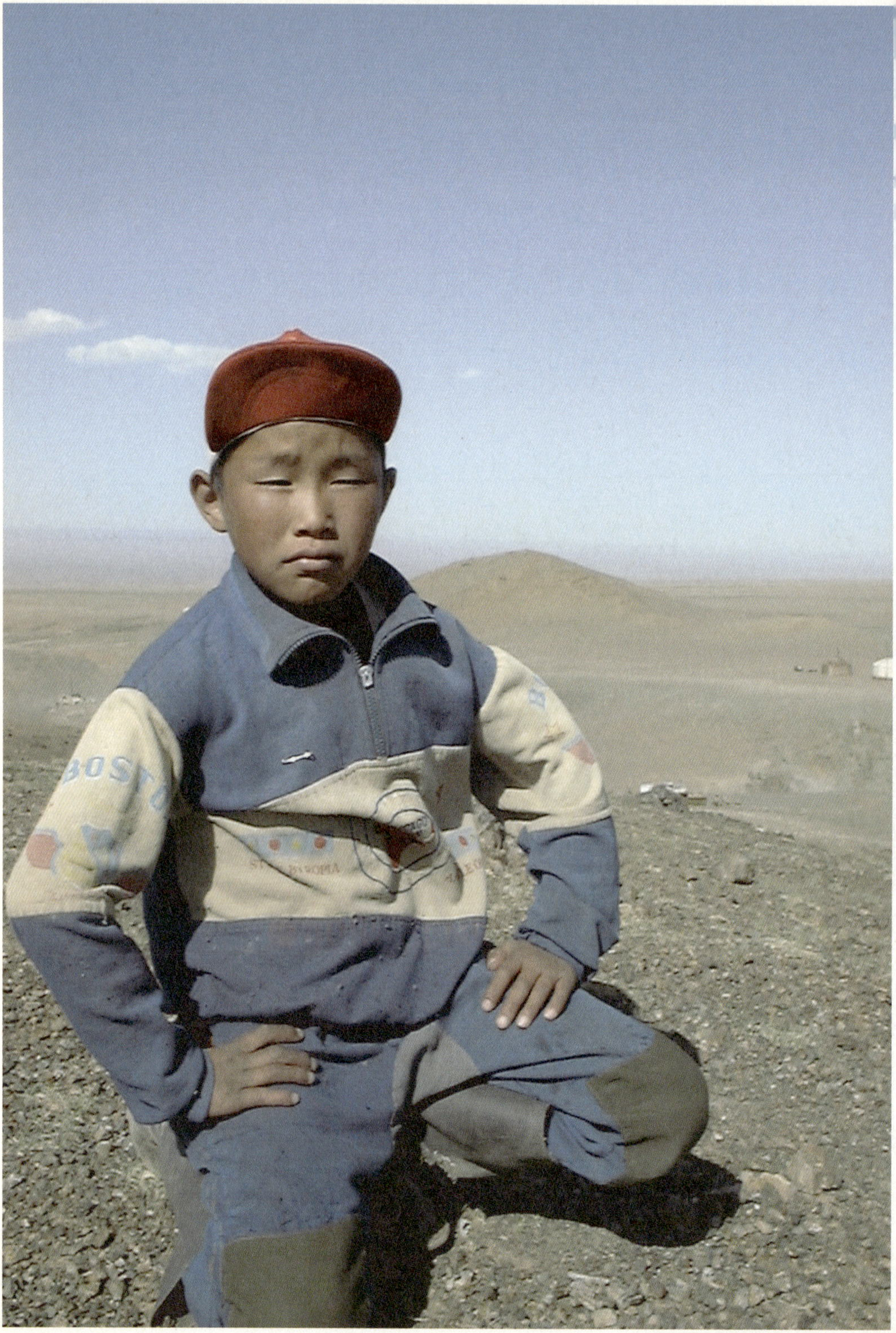

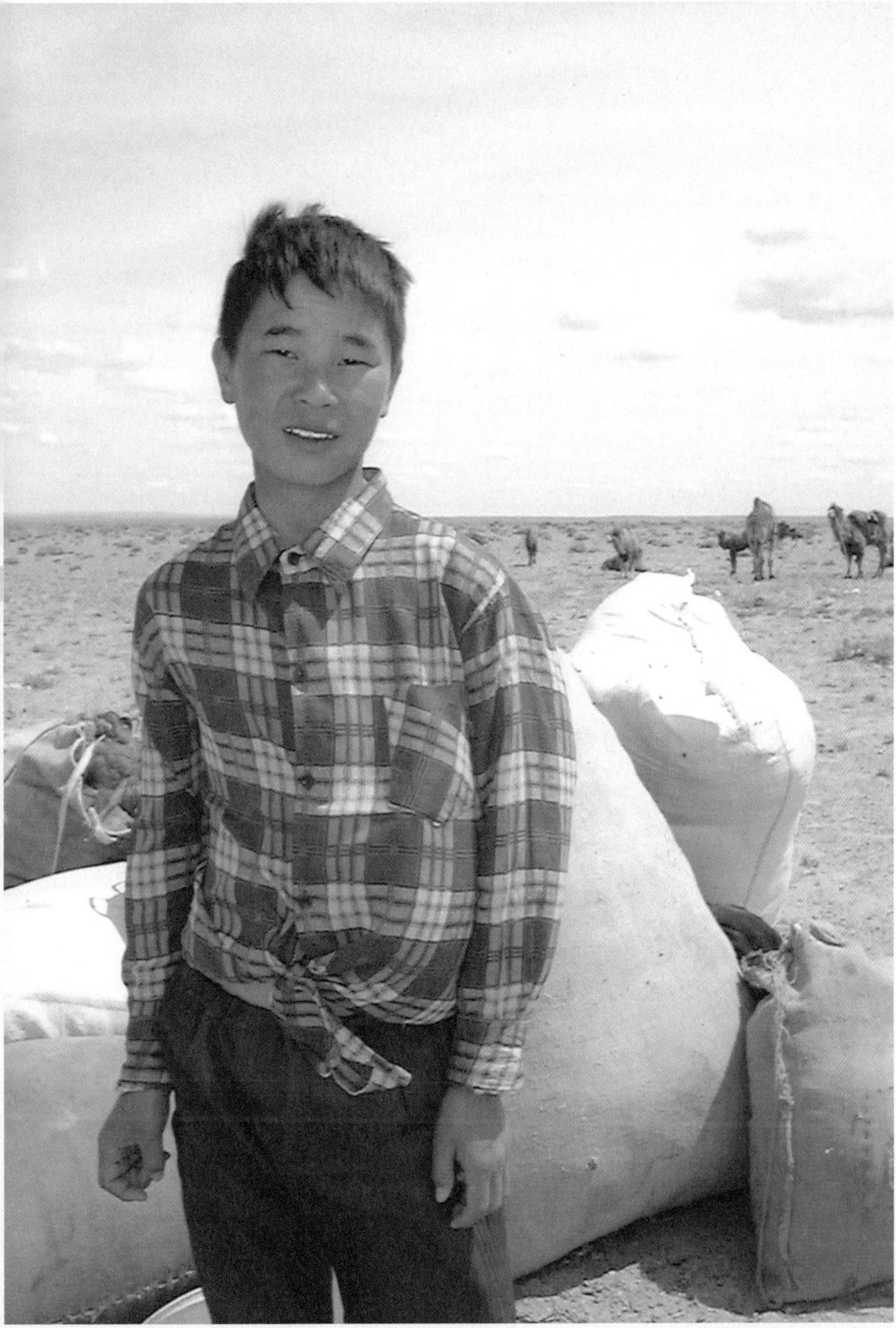

シベリア鉄道

シベリア鉄道の幅65センチの寝台に寝ころびながら、
2日も3日も延々と続く牧歌的なホノボノ風景に目を滑らせる。

「世界の車窓から」じゃないけど、窓の外の景色なんて5分も見れば充分！
電車のゆったり旅なんて50年早かった。
もう暇で暇で電車中を何度も走り回って、タイムを計りたくなっちゃう。

こんな暇なときは、ずっと持ち歩いているグッズが大活躍。
CDウォークマンとミニスピーカー、ミニラジカセ、そして厳選された48枚のCD。
日本で買い込んだ文庫本十数冊。
デジカメ、デジビデ、ノートパソコン。
そして、バックパッカーズギターとハーモニカ数本。
スケッチブックとクレヨンセット....
もうほとんど、「動く自分の部屋」状態。

ガイドブックには「軽い荷物が旅を楽しむコツうんたらかんたら」なんて書いてあるけど、オレは反対。
持てる限界まで遊び道具をいっぱいいっぱい詰め込んで、世界をハッピーに放浪してる。

だって、「このシチュエーションでこの曲を聞きたい！この本を読みたい！絵を描きたい！唄いたい！....」とかって、めちゃめちゃ大事じゃん。
それに比べたら、移動のときのバックパックの重さなんて、眼中ないよ。

Siberian Railroad

As I lay in the 65cm width of the Siberian Railroad's sleeping carriage,
my eyes slide along the warm, pastoral scenery that continues endlessly for 2 or 3 days.

It's not the TV program "See the World by Train",
but five minutes of the scenery from the window is more than enough.
I was 50 years too young for a relaxing trip by train.
Bored completely out of my mind to the point I've run through the train so many times,
I almost want to time myself.

In times like this, the goods I've been carrying around with me the whole time plays a big role..
a CD walkman and mini speakers
a mini radio/cassette player
and 48 carefully selected CDs
a dozen or so paperbacks I bought in Japan
digital camera, digital video camera, laptop
also, a backpacker's guitar and a couple of harmonicas
a sketch book and a set of crayons
practically like "my portable room"

In guidebooks, "The lighter your pack, the better the trip...blah, blah, blah,"
They write, but I oppose.
I've packed in lots and lots of toys, as much as I can possibly carry, and am roaming the world happily.

Because, if ever, "I want to listen to this song in this situation!" or "I want to read this book right here!" or "Want to draw a picture!" or "Want to sing!"...that's soooooo important.
Compared to that, the weight of my pack when on the road means nothing.

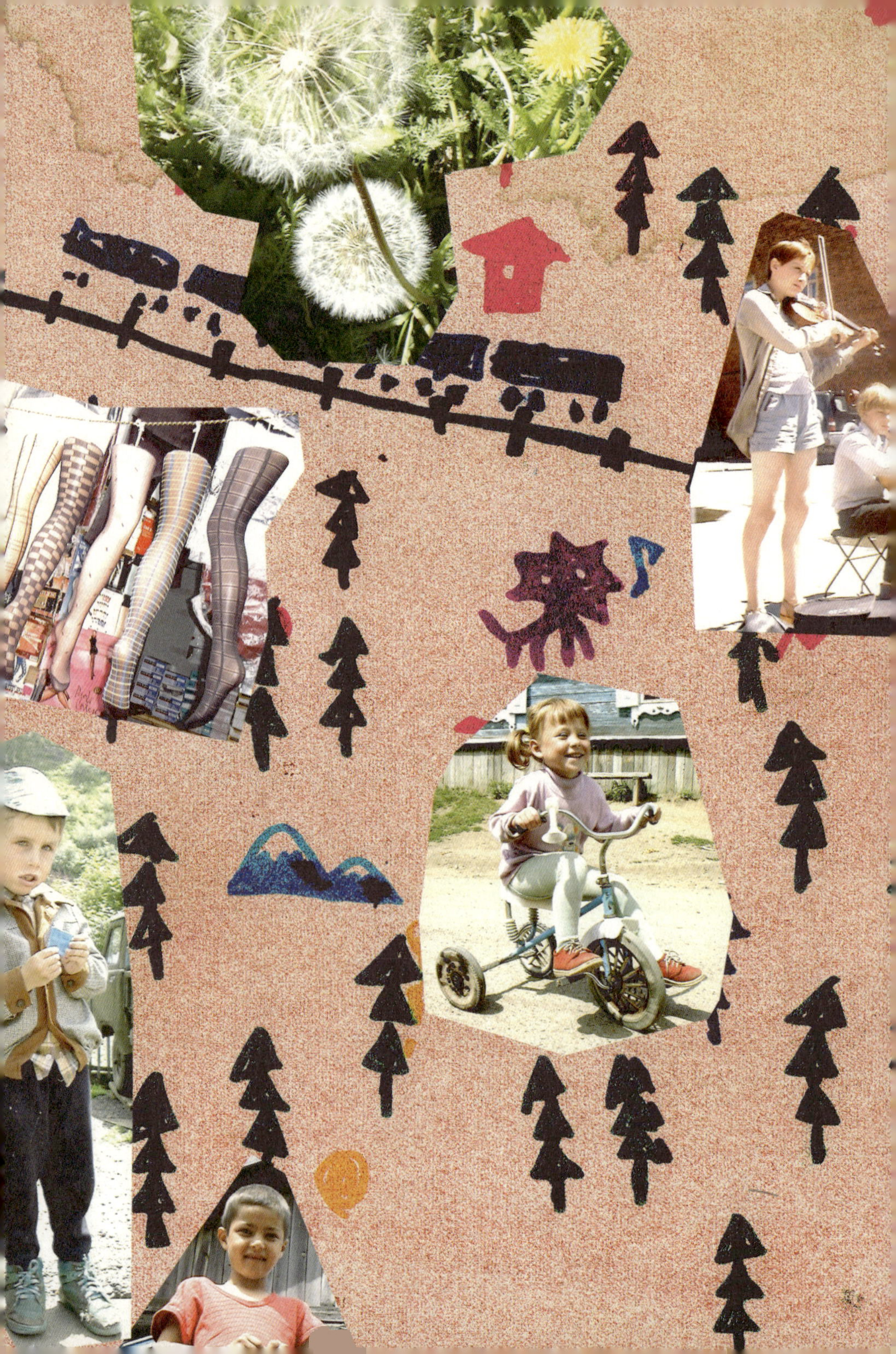

LOVE

サヤカの手

シベリア鉄道を途中下車して寄った、イルクーツク。
ロシアの小さな街はずれで過ごす、ふたりだけの静かな午後。
古い教会の鐘、路面電車、荷馬車、木々や小鳥たちが無意識に奏でるBGM。
お互いに黙ったままでも、時間は穏やかに流れる。

なにげなく「サヤカの手」を撮ってみた。

へぇ～、こんな手をしてたんだぁ。

6年以上も一緒にいて、今まで何千回も目にはしていたけど、
サヤカの手を「見た」のは、初めてだった。

結構、オレ、この女性のこと知らないんだなぁ。

意外で新鮮な感じと、ちょっと申し訳ないような感じが入り混じって、
妙に複雑な気分。

オレは、この女性のことをどれくらい知っているんだろう？
この女性は、オレのことをどのくらい知っているんだろう？

Sayaka's Hand

stopping off the Siberian Railroad at Irkutsk
on the edges of a small town we spend
just the two of us, a quiet afternoon
a bell of an old church, a streetcar, a wagon,
the trees and small birds...
unconsciously become back ground music
although we are both silent, time flows peacefully

Without thinking, I took "Sayaka's hand."

Wow...is this the kind of hand she had?

Although we'd been together for more than 6 years
I'd seen her hands thousands of times
I was "looking" at Sayaka's hand for the very first time

There's quite a lot I don't know about this woman

Mixed with an unexpectedly fresh feeling and a little
bit of guilt
A really strange, complicated feeling

I wonder, how much of this woman do I really know?
I wonder, how much does this woman really know about me?

モスクワで。眠れぬ夜に。

オレは昔から「ヤンキー」であり、「優等生」だった。
茶髪長ランでビーバップしながら、家では進研ゼミとかやってるような奴だった。

今も「ロックだぜ！ビートだぜ！ドロップアウトだぜ！面倒なことは考えずにハッピーにやろうぜ！」っていう自分もホントだし、
「優しさってなんだろう」「幸せってなんだろう」「満員電車に吐き出されて団地に帰っていくサラリーマンオヤジの背中にも男を感じるよなぁ」．．．．．なんてことをマジに考えるオレもホントだと思う。

一見矛盾しそうないくつもの極端なキャラクターが、オレの中で仲良く同居し続けてる。
「西郷隆盛リードボーカルのロックバンド」「長渕剛監督のディズニー映画」「ダライラマ＆星野道夫主演のイージーライダー」．．．．．なんていうイメージが好き！というオレのスタイル。

疲れているのに、なぜか眠れない夜。
そんな事をもにょもにょとオモイながら、
モスクワの安ホテルのベッドに転がっているオレ。

A Sleepless Night in Moscow

I have always been a "punk", and at the same time,
a "good student".
Be-bopping around with unacceptable haircuts and
clothing, but at home I studied my ass off, alone.

Even now, when I say things like "Rock! Beat! Dropouts!
Don't think too much, let's be happy!"...that's the
real me. And when I think seriously, "What is true
kindness? What is true happiness?...that's the
real me, too.

Different extreme characters that would contradict
each other, are at peace with each other within me.
"Lead vocal, Saigo Takamori's rock band", "Director,
Nagabuchi Tsuyoshi's Disney movie", "Easy Rider starring
the Dalai Lama and Hoshino Michio"...
These images I like. This is my style.

Tonight I am tired but for some reason cannot sleep.
I think of these things restlessly.
Tossing and turning in a cheap hotel room bed in Moscow.

ガラクタに、愛を。

Love For Junk.

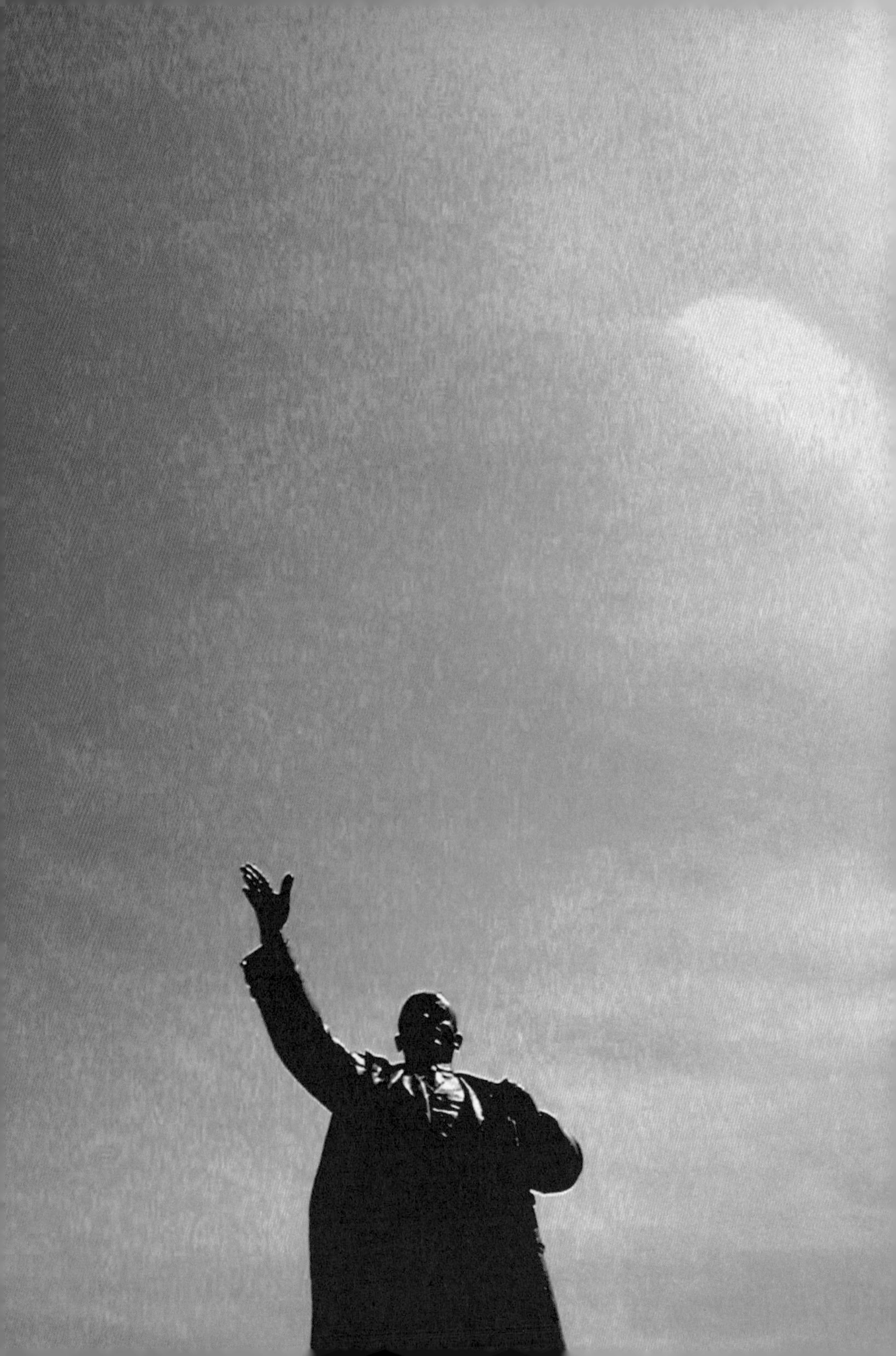

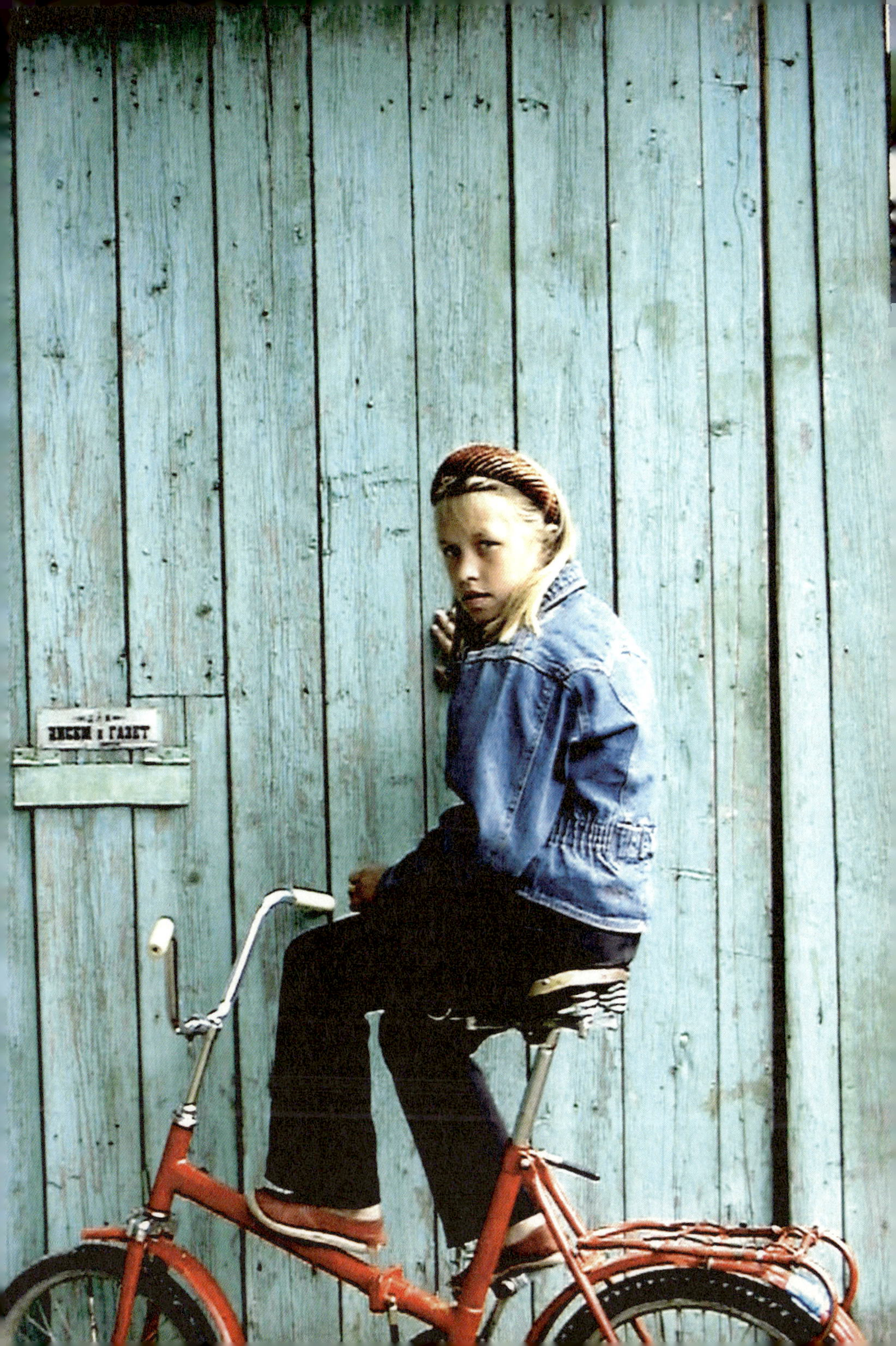

フィンランドにて

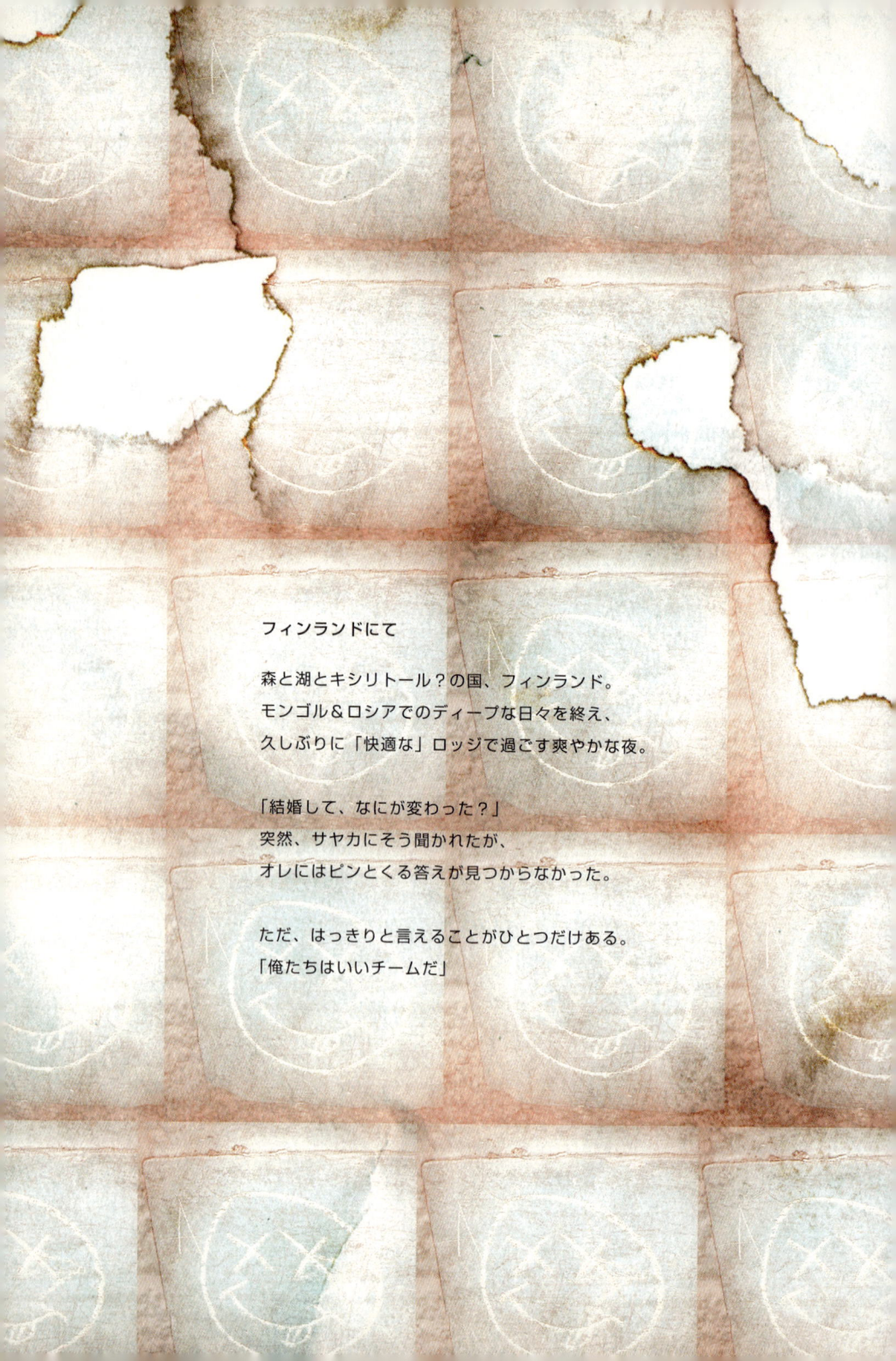

森と湖とキシリトール？の国、フィンランド。
モンゴル＆ロシアでのディープな日々を終え、
久しぶりに「快適な」ロッジで過ごす爽やかな夜。

「結婚して、なにが変わった？」
突然、サヤカにそう聞かれたが、
オレにはピンとくる答えが見つからなかった。

ただ、はっきりと言えることがひとつだけある。
「俺たちはいいチームだ」

In Finland

The land of woods, lakes, and xylitol? Finland.
Following the deep days spent in Mongolia and Russia,
The first fresh night in a "comfortable" lodge in a
long time.

"Has anything changed since we've been married?"
Sayaka asked out of the blue.
I couldn't find the right answer.

But, there is one thing I am absolutely sure of.
"We make a good team!"

2％のツバ

人と逢っても、本を読んでも、写真集を見ても、BARで飲んでも、
映画を見ても、音楽を聴いても、建物を見ても、イベントに行っても....
悔しいくらい、世界中に「スゴイヒト」「スゴイサクヒン」は溢れている。

「こりゃ、すげぇや！」とココロが震えるとき、
俺は98％の感動の後、2％のツバを吐く。
「オレも絶対負けねぇぞ」
そのツバの中に、明日の俺がいるから。

でも、不思議だ。
「大自然のスゴサ」にだけは100％とろ〜んって溶けちゃうんだよな。

2% Spit

Meeting people, reading books, seeing photographs,
drinking in bars, watching movies, listening to music,
seeing architecture, or going to events...
It's almost annoying how many "GREAT People" or
"GREAT Works" there are overflowing in this world.

When my heart flutters, "Wow...This is awesome!"
After I am impressed 98%, I spit 2%.
"I, too, will never be defeated."
In the spit, is my motivation for tomorrow.

But, it's odd.
Only to "GREATNESS of Nature", I melt 100%.

シンプル

世界放浪を続けているうちに、
大事なことがどんどんシンプルになってきた。

大きなもの、広いもの、多種多様なものに触れれば触れるほど、
大事なことは小さく小さく絞られていく気がする。

おやじ、おふくろ、弟、妹、彼女、仲間....
「大切な誰か」のために始めた小さなことが、
結果として大きな世界を HAPPY にしていくことになる。

Simple

continuing to roam the world
the important things become more and more simple

big things, spacious things, the more variety of
things I come in contact with
the finer and finer the important things tend to
come into focus

Dad, Mom, brother, sister, wife, friends...
that small something I started for "someone special"
in the end will make the big world HAPPY

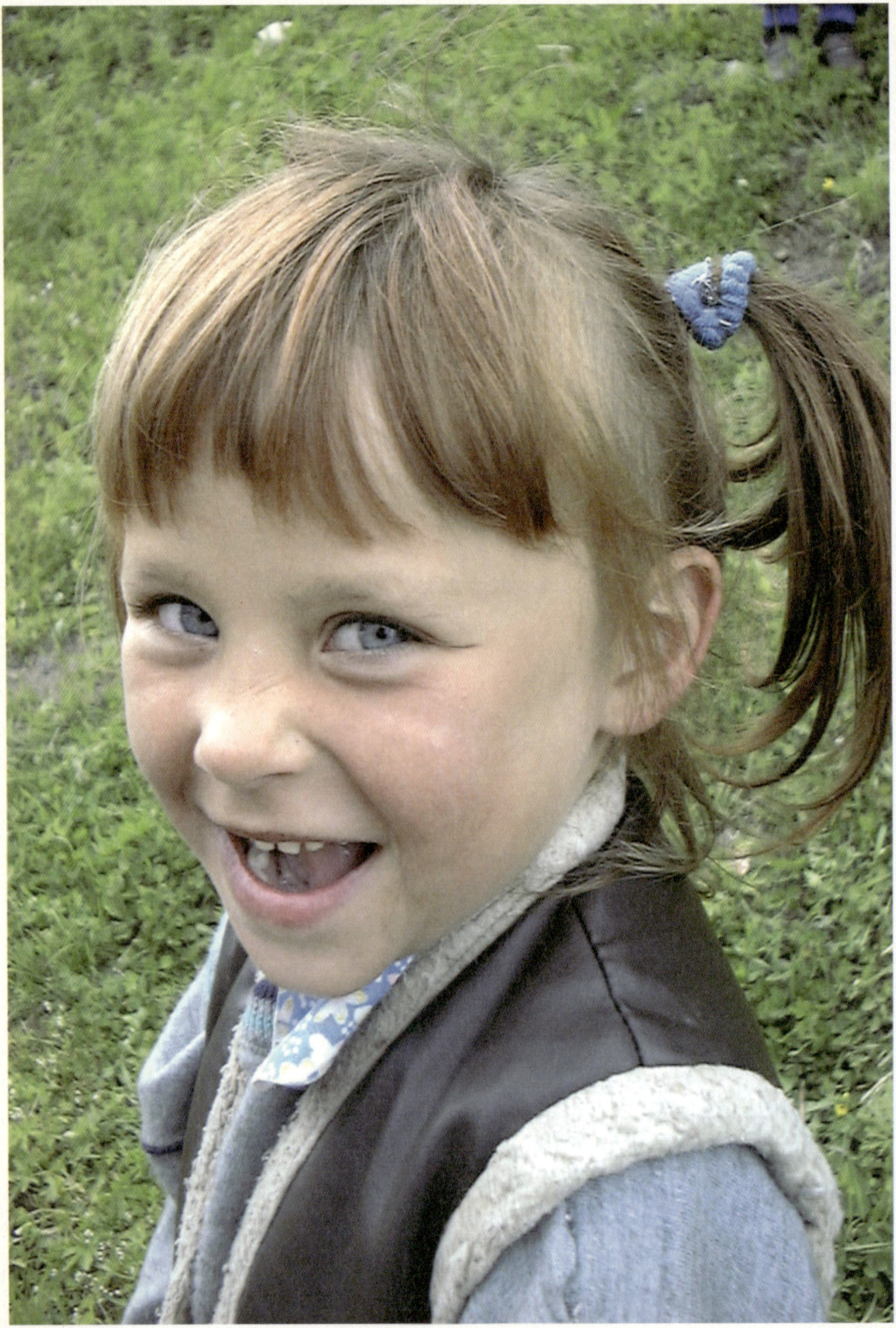

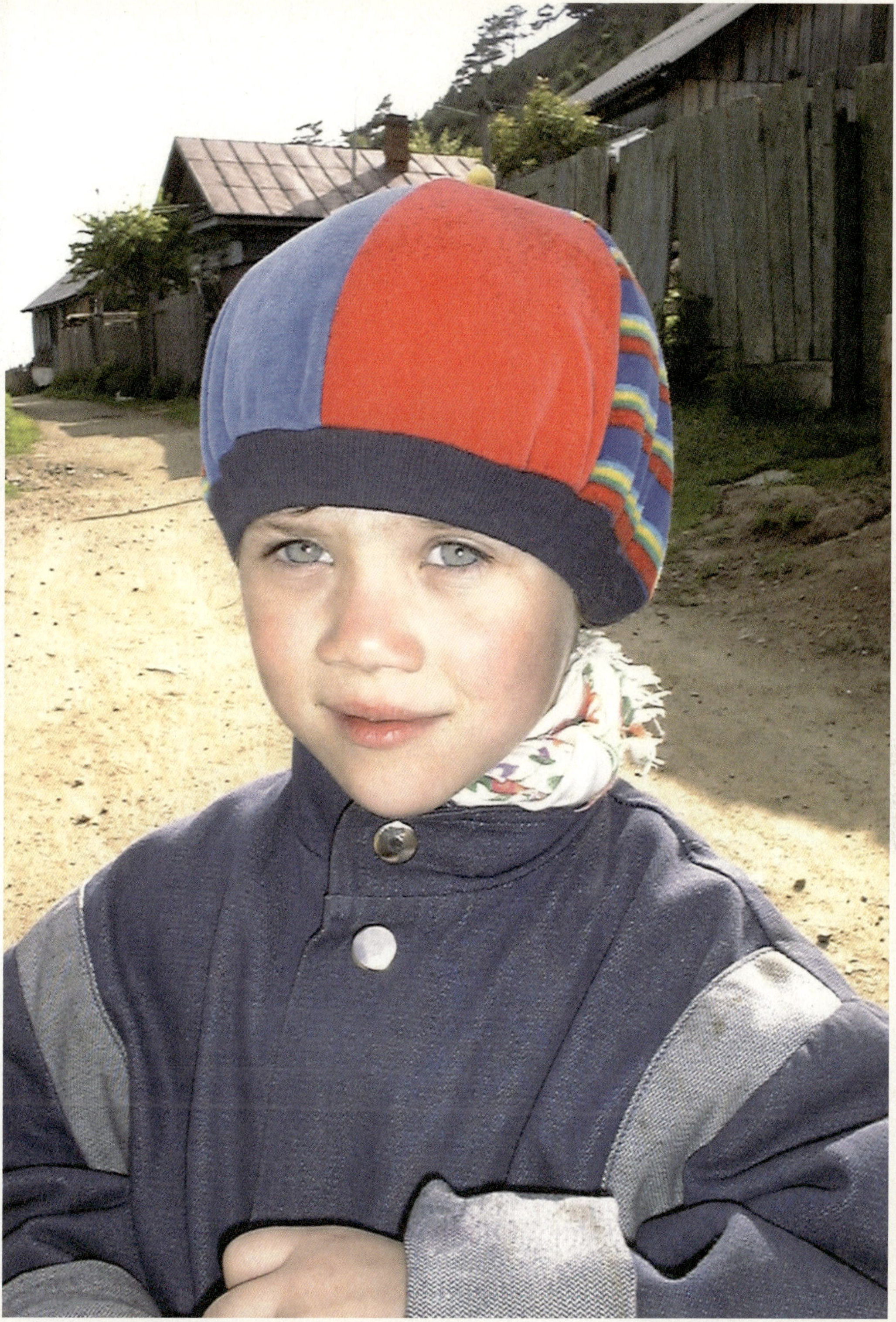

Journey 4 :

Eur

ope

プライド

旅を続けながら、どこに行っても誰に逢っても、オレがオレであり続けられることに、自信を持ててきた。

ただひとつ。
世界中の同世代の奴らと語っていて、
いつも「負けた！」と思うことがある。
それは、「自分の国への誇り」だ。

世界を放浪してると、自分が日本人であることを「実感」する。
そして、日本人なのに日本のことを全然知らない自分に驚く。
恋人や映画の話をするのと同じテンションで、ナチュラルに自分の国の政治や歴史について語る各国の同世代の奴らといると、
なんだか同じ地球の上に暮らしている人間として、
自分は地に足がついていない気がして、
正直、ちょっと悔しくなるときがある。

やっぱり、オレは日本人なんだし、「日本的なもの」を知って、愛して、誇りを持つことは、人間として自然だと思う。
「自分の国の歴史や現実」についての話を「堅い話」とチャカしたり、
「愛国心」みたいなものを「右翼」とか言って変にタブーにするのは、逆に不自然な気がしてきている。

そんなわけで、最近は路上に座り込んでコーラ片手にタバコを吹かしながら、日本の歴史の本にハマっています。
でもさぁ、おもしろいね、日本史って。
「日本史？うぜぇよ」なんて言って、いつも授業をバックれていた高校時代の先生に逢わす顔がないよ。
スダセンセイ、ゴメンね。

Pride

Continuing my journey, no matter where I go or
who I meet, I've become confident that I can
continue being myself.

Except for one thing.
Talking to people of my generation, all over the world,
There's always one thing that makes me feel like
"I've been beaten."
That is, "Pride in one's own country."

Roaming the world, it makes me "realize" that
I am a Japanese.
Yet, I am shocked that I don't know anything about
Japan, although I am Japanese.
In the same tone as if they were discussing
relationships or movies,
Being with people of my generation from various
countries that speak naturally about politics or
history of their country.
As a person living on the same planet,
Somehow, I feel as if my feet are not on the ground,
Truthfully, at times I am a little ashamed.

After all, I am Japanese,
To know and love and have pride in "Japanese-ish things"
I feel is natural as a human.
Joking around that discussions about "history or
current issues of one's country" are "too serious" or
strangely creating a taboo that things like "patriotism"
somehow is "right-winged" actually has started to
seem unnatural.

possono aiutarti a
smettere di fumare

4 mg Nicotina
0,4 mg
CO 5 mg

PAGATO

PAGATO

VA IN SCENA LA DARK L

L'associazione culturale
Valentina Moncada ha intitolato
Giallo d'Autore la mostra dedi-
cata alle creazioni di moda di Jean
Paul Najar e ai celebri scatti
fotografici di Roberto Opianca
di altri fotografi dell'epoca. Tu
nere capaci di rendere corpi sa
a linee filiformi, forme primario di
colori dal forte contrasto, cappelli
e abiti sculture tra Capucci e
Rodchenko, sono le creazioni
sartoriali di Jean Paul Najar,
accoppiate alle imm

That's why, lately, I sit on the streets with a Coke in one hand, smoking a cigarette, completely hooked on Japanese history books.
But you know...Japanese history is really interesting.
"Japanese history? Boring!" I'd said,
always skipping class back in high school.
Too embarrassed of myself to face that teacher now.
Sorry, Mr. Suda.

Film

L'IMPORTANZA DI CHIAMARSI FLUI⑤
Lorenzo Conte, Edoardo

闘いの前夜には、人生の主題歌を唄え。

Sing life's theme song,
the night before a conflict.

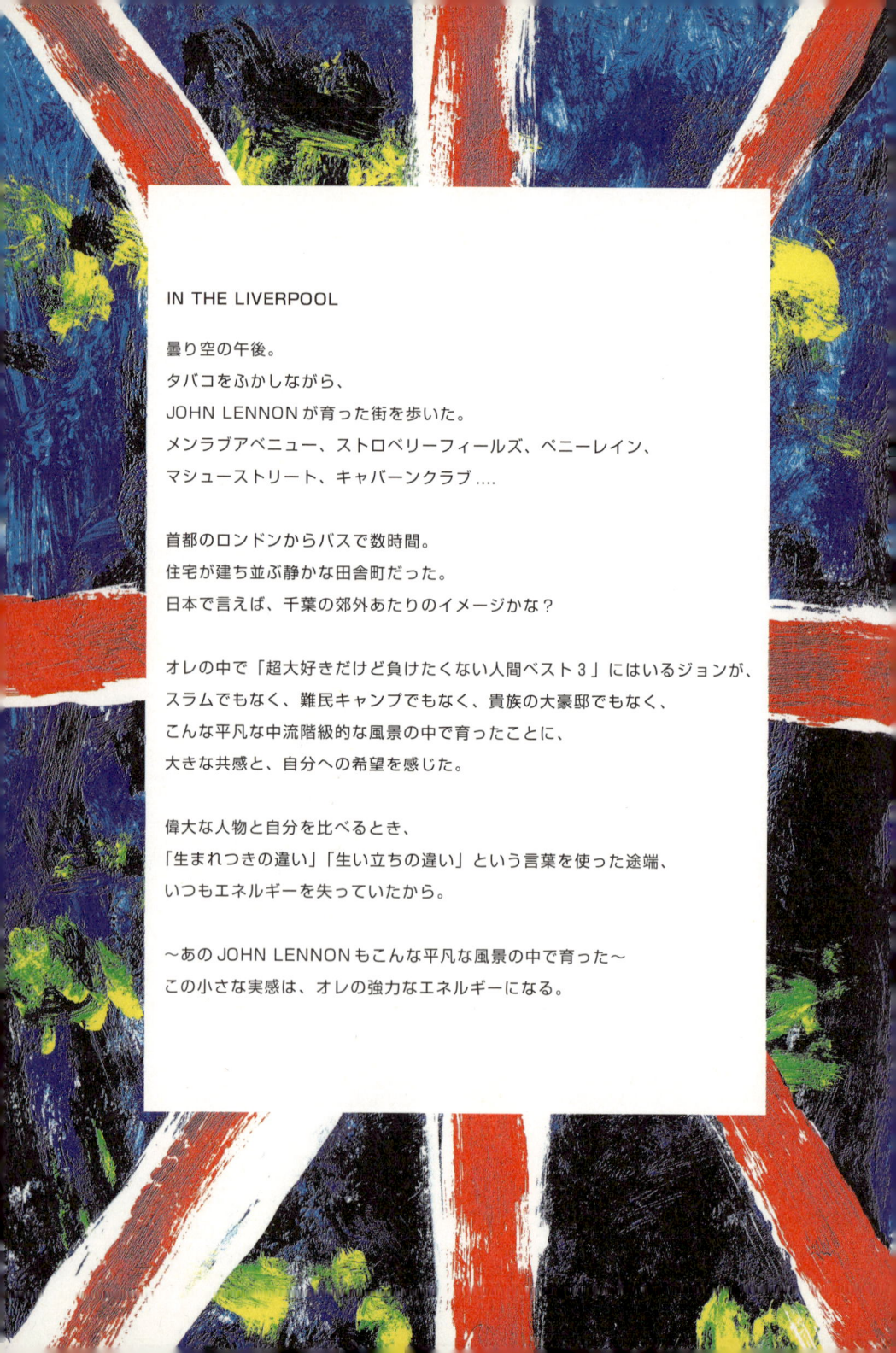

IN THE LIVERPOOL

曇り空の午後。
タバコをふかしながら、
JOHN LENNONが育った街を歩いた。
メンラブアベニュー、ストロベリーフィールズ、ペニーレイン、
マシューストリート、キャバーンクラブ....

首都のロンドンからバスで数時間。
住宅が建ち並ぶ静かな田舎町だった。
日本で言えば、千葉の郊外あたりのイメージかな？

オレの中で「超大好きだけど負けたくない人間ベスト３」にはいるジョンが、
スラムでもなく、難民キャンプでもなく、貴族の大豪邸でもなく、
こんな平凡な中流階級的な風景の中で育ったことに、
大きな共感と、自分への希望を感じた。

偉大な人物と自分を比べるとき、
「生まれつきの違い」「生い立ちの違い」という言葉を使った途端、
いつもエネルギーを失っていたから。

〜あのJOHN LENNONもこんな平凡な風景の中で育った〜
この小さな実感は、オレの強力なエネルギーになる。

In the Liverpool

a cloudy afternoon
smoking a cigarette
I walked the streets where John Lennon grew up
Menlove Avenue, Strawberry Field, Penny Lane,
Mathew Street, Cavern Club...

a few hours by bus from London
a quiet country town lined with houses
in Japan, maybe...equivalent to Chiba's suburbs?

John, to me, one of the "Top 3 people I exceptionally
admire but don't want to lose to"
grew up not in the slums, not in a refugee camp,
not in a mansion of royalty
but in such an ordinary, middle class type neighborhood
I could really relate, and it gave me hope.

when comparing myself to someone great
as soon as I used the words "innate differences" or
"lifestyle differences"
I would always lose ENERGY

"That John Lennon grew up in such an ordinary world, too."
This small realization will become a huge ENERGY for me.

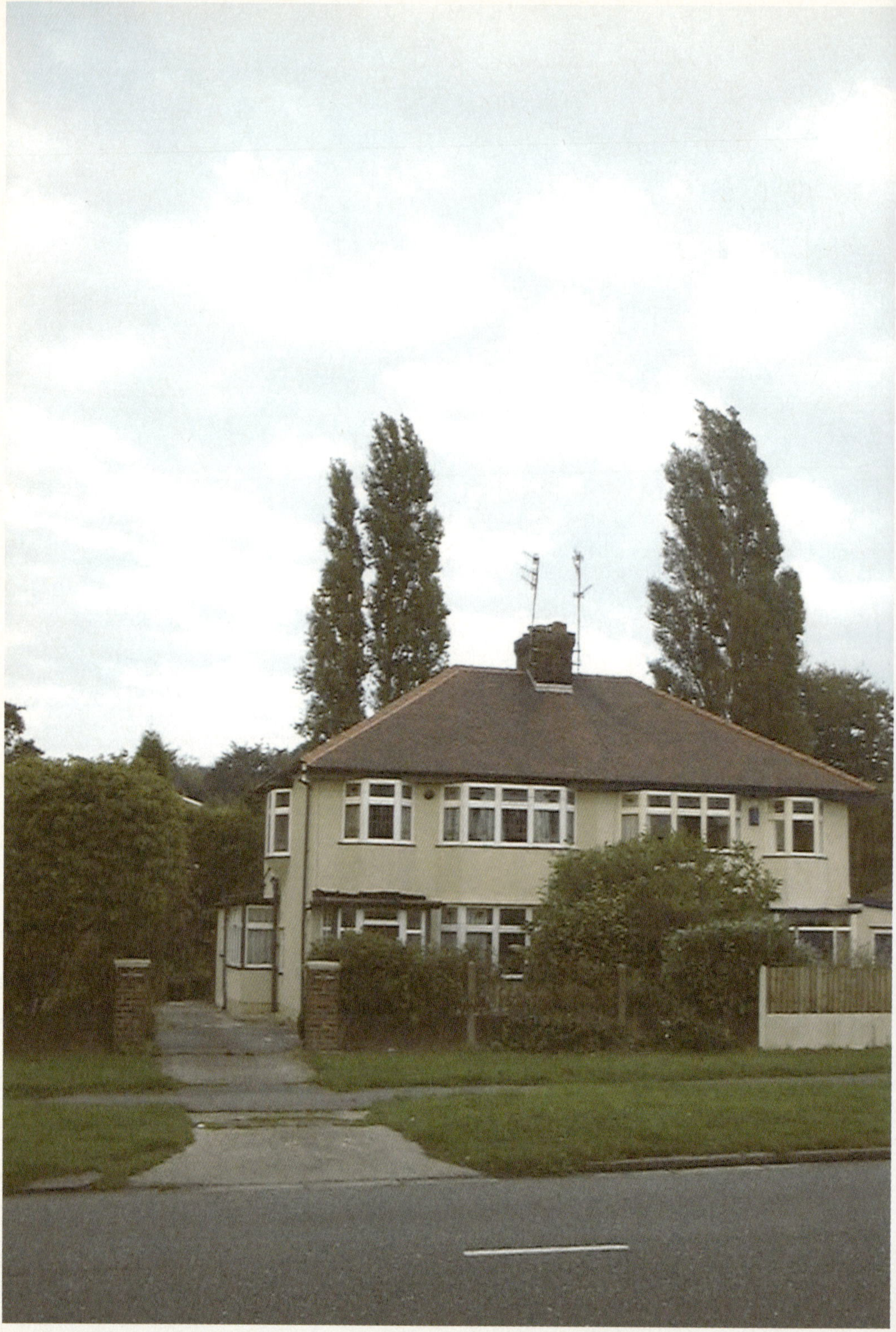

251

The
CAVERN
CLUB
THE CAVERN
THE CAVERN

STRAWBERRY
FIELD
ABBY
KELLY

偉大なる作品は、彼女の寝顔によって生まれる。

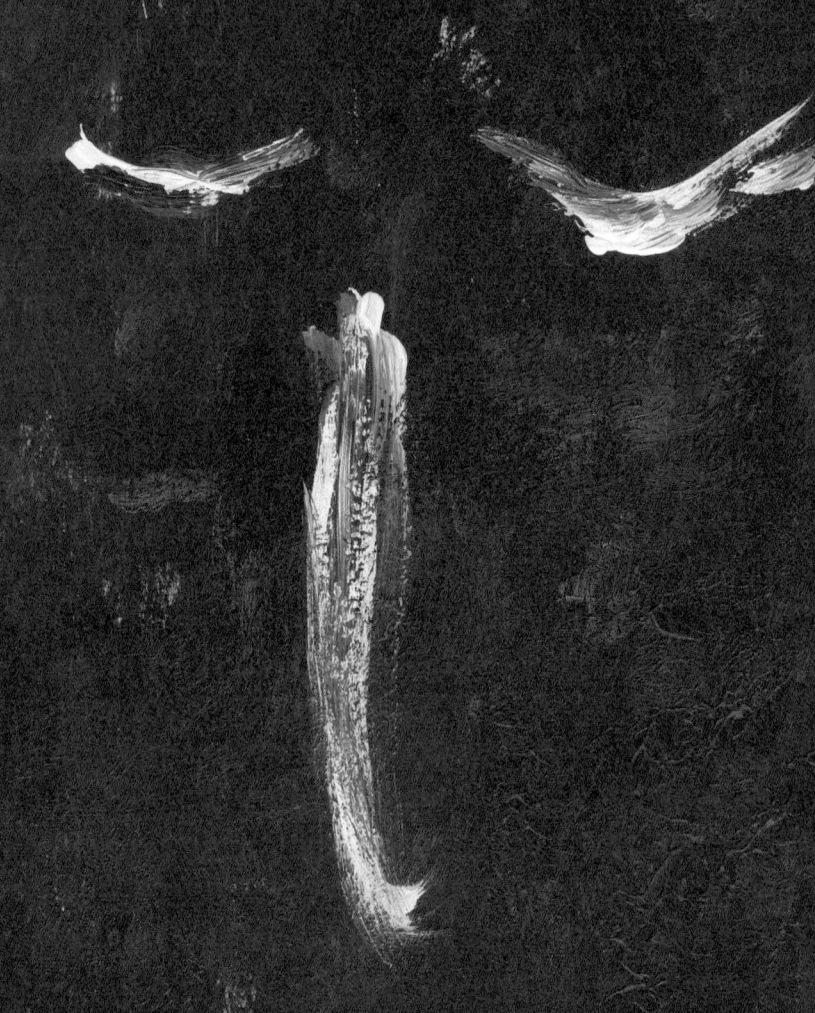

Through her sleeping face,
great works will come to life.

たまに、「もうひとりのオレ」が自分に問いかけてくる。

日本も含め世界中でこんなに苦しんでいる人がいるというのに、
オマエは自分の楽しみばかりを追求して生きていて本当にいいのか？
何か、オマエにも果たさなければいけない「役割」があるんじゃないのか？

でもね。

ボランティアや寄付や慈善活動だけが、他人の役に立ってるわけじゃない。
人にはそれぞれの役割がある。
みんなが、それぞれ自分自身のココロの声に正直に、
やるべきことを一生懸命にやればいい。

オレは、オレの大好きなことを通して、オレを表現し続けるだけ。

それが、結果として誰かの役に立てばサイコーだと思ってる。

Sometimes, "the other me" asks.

So many people in this world, including Japan,
are suffering,
Yet, are you sure it's really right to live
pursuing only your own pleasures?
Isn't there some "role" you should be fulfilling?

But...

Volunteer work, donations, and charity aren't the
only things that serve others.
Everyone has his own role.
Everyone honestly listens to the voice of his own heart,
And does what he should with all his might, that's fine.

As for me, through the things I love, I will just
continue to express myself.

If that, as a result, serves someone in someway,
that would be great!

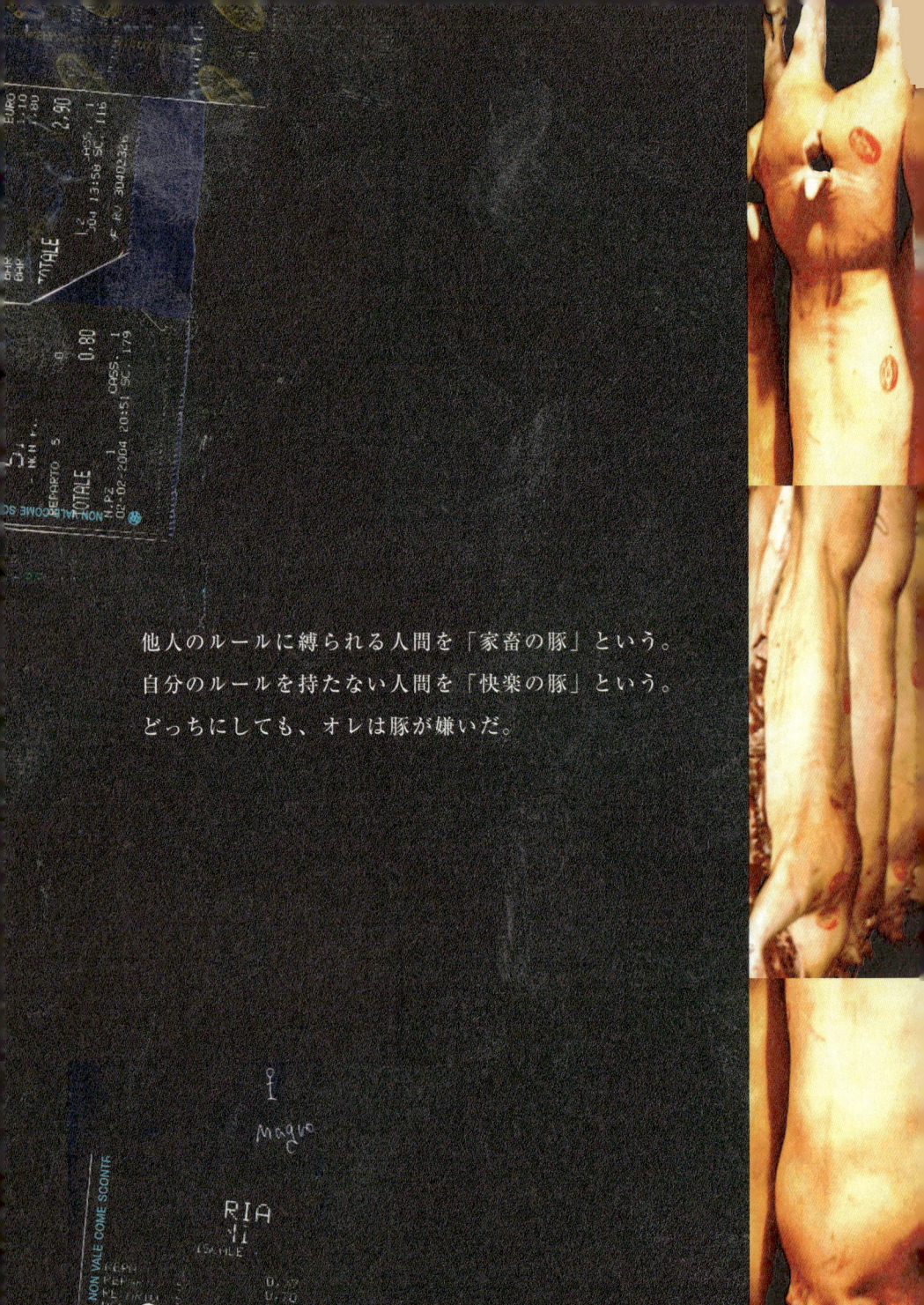

他人のルールに縛られる人間を「家畜の豚」という。
自分のルールを持たない人間を「快楽の豚」という。
どっちにしても、オレは豚が嫌いだ。

Those who are restrained by other people's rules are called "pigs of livestock".
Those who do not have their own rules are called "pigs of pleasure".
Either way, I hate pigs.

EVERY BREATH YOU TAKE

旅を続けて約1年間。
オレタチふたりは、ほぼ24時間、お互い「3メートル以内の距離」で
暮らしていた。
24時間×365日＝8760時間！
治安のいい場所でたまに別行動する時間を差し引いても、約8000時間。
よく考えると、これは凄いことだ。
日本で暮らす忙しい夫婦だったとしたら、いったい何年分に値するんだろう？
これだけ長い間、ひとりの人間と真っ正面から向き合って過ごしたのは初めてだ。

悪人や病気を退治しつつ、コトバや習慣もまったくわからない国々を渡り歩き、
ふたりの楽しみを互いに尊重しながら一緒に泣いたり笑ったり。
もちろんケンカもしまくりだけど、宿の小さな部屋にふたり、お互いに逃げ場所
がないから本音トークの嵐。
オレの得意だったハッタリやカッコつけなんて一切通用しない状況で、ちょっと
大げさに言えば、どこまで「惚れるに値する男でいられるか」の真価が問われる
日々だ。

週に一回デートしてた頃は、「かっこいい男」でいるのは簡単だったけど、
今は結構大変。
自信がない奴は、くれぐれも彼女と長旅をしないように。
かなり、ヘビーだぜ。

Every Breath You Take

On the road for about a year.
We as a couple, for practically 24 hours a day, have been living "within 3 meters distance" of each other.
24 hours a day x 365 days = 8760 hours!!
Even if we subtract the time we spent apart in safe areas, that's still about 8000 hours.
If you really think about it, this is quite amazing.
If this were a busy couple living in Japan, how many years time would that be equivalent to?
It's the first time ever I've spent such a long time directly facing just one person.

Getting through dangerous people and diseases, going from country to country where the language and customs are completely different, respecting each other's pleasures, together we cried and we laughed.
Of course we have had our share of fights, but with no place for either of us to hide, the two of us in the small hotel room we share, storms of heart-to heart talks.
In situations where the bluffing and tough-guy-act I was so good at, not working at all, exaggerating just a little, they were days of challenging the true worth of "How much longer I can be a man worthy of your love."

Back when we were out on dates once a week, it was easy to be the "cool guy".
But now,
It's pretty tough.
For those guys who don't have much confidence, be sure never to take long trips with your girlfriend.
It's pretty heavy stuff.

RESTAURANTE LEON

Km 33

Classe

REG

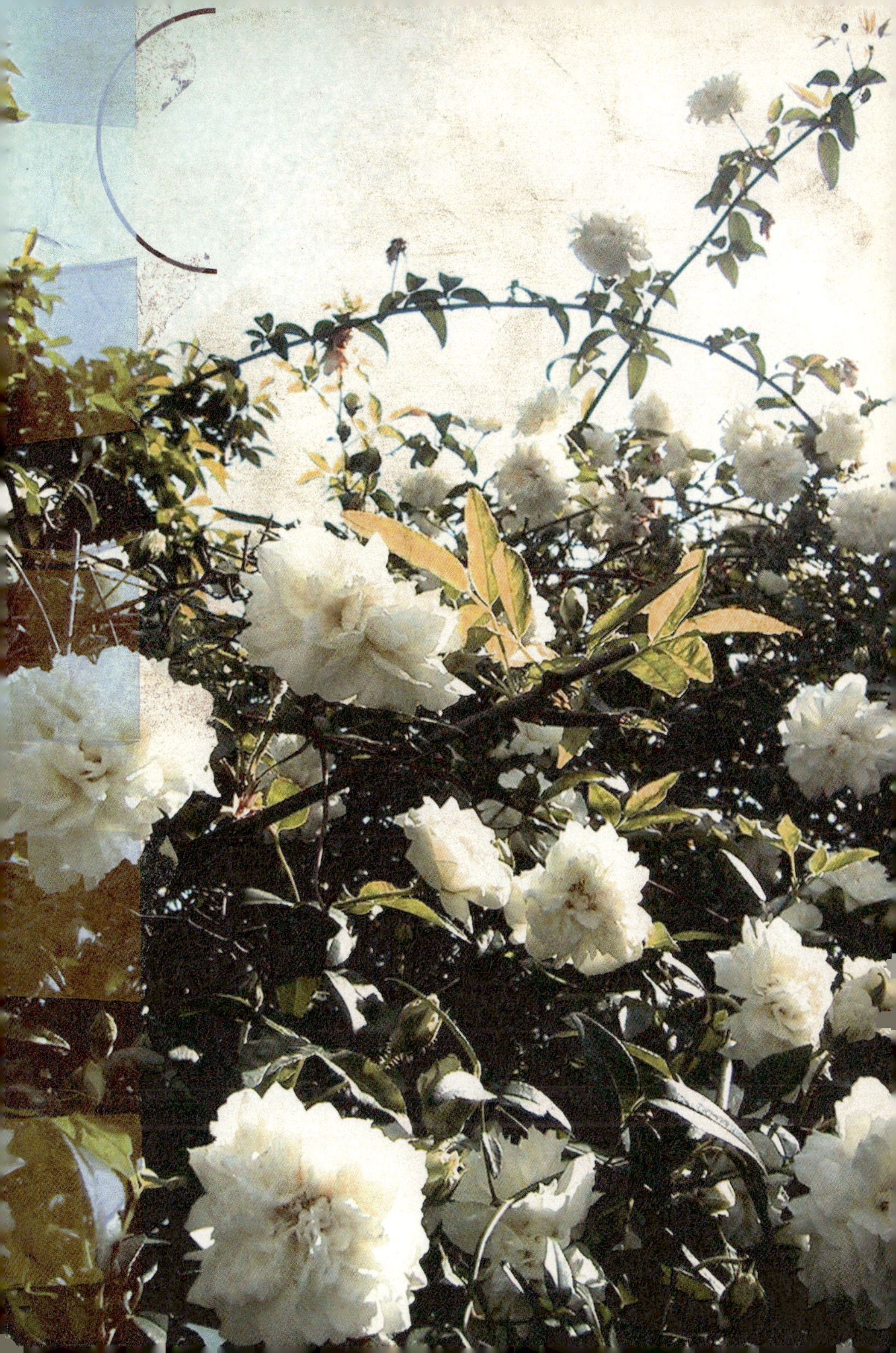

心ある仕事

心ないボランティアよりも、心あるバーテンダーのほうが、
世の中の役に立っていることが多い。

心ない政治家よりも、心ある掃除のおばちゃんのほうが、
世の中の役に立っていることが多い。

「心ある仕事」をしている人は、みんな世の中の役に立っているんだ。

世界中の路地を歩きながら、たまにそんなことを考える。

Job with Heart

compared to a volunteer without heart
a bartender with heart
often is more helpful in the real world

compared to a politician without heart
a janitor lady with heart
often is more helpful in the real world

everyone doing a "Job with Heart"
is useful in the real world

walking the streets of the world
I sometimes think of these things

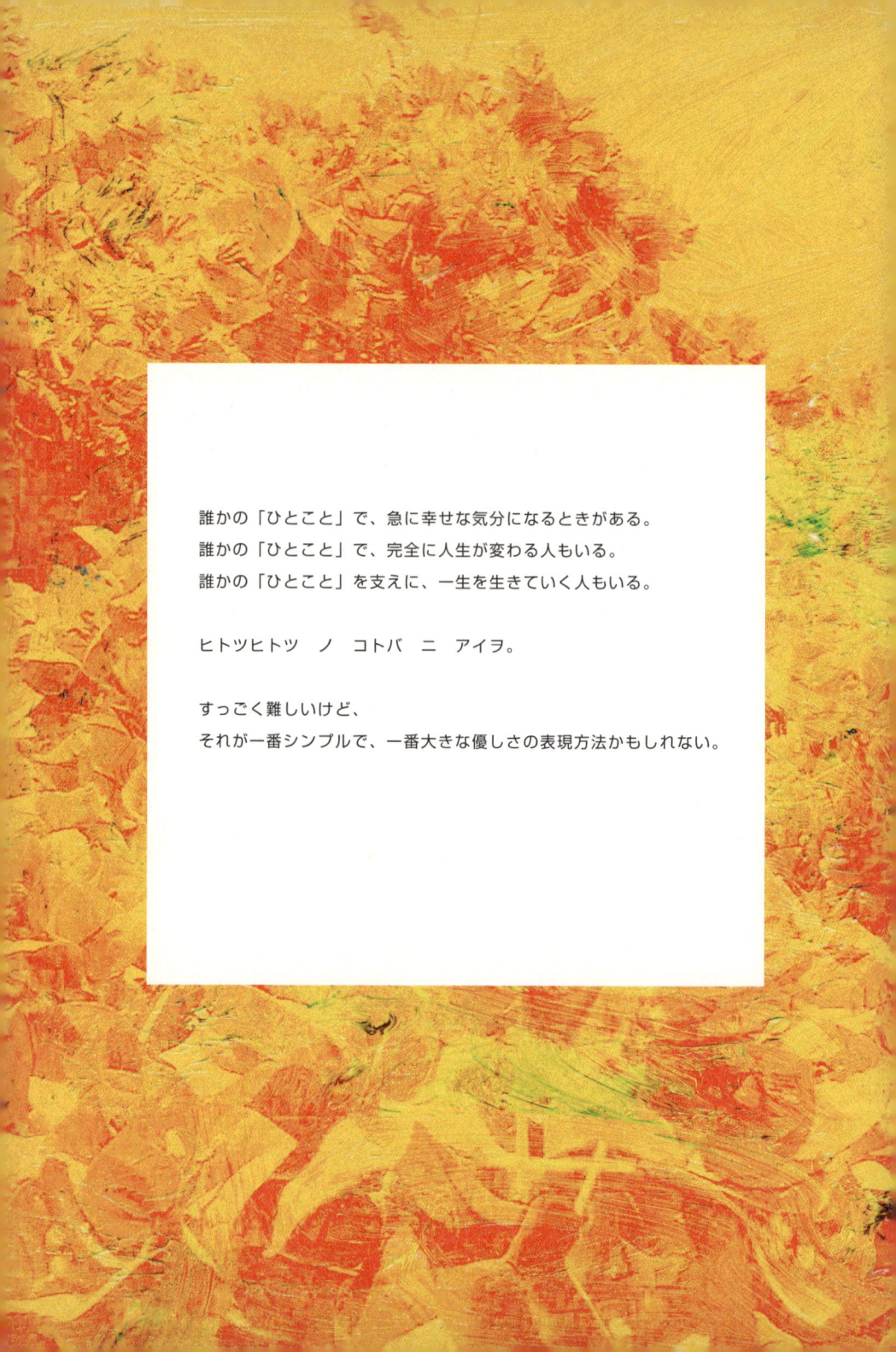

誰かの「ひとこと」で、急に幸せな気分になるときがある。
誰かの「ひとこと」で、完全に人生が変わる人もいる。
誰かの「ひとこと」を支えに、一生を生きていく人もいる。

ヒトツヒトツ　ノ　コトバ　ニ　アイヲ。

すっごく難しいけど、
それが一番シンプルで、一番大きな優しさの表現方法かもしれない。

With someone's "one word",
there are times one can suddenly become happy.
With someone's "one word",
there are people whose lives are completely changed.
As someone's "one word" for support,
there are people who will live their whole lives.

WITH LOVE TO EACH AND EVERY "ONE WORD"

It's really hard to do, but...
It's the most simple, and possibly the biggest
expression of kindness there is.

一生懸命、相談にのってくれてありがとう。
でも、ワタシが知りたかったのは、「あなたの答え」ではないみたい。
きっと、「ワタシが考える手伝い」をして欲しかっただけなの。

アイツの瞳が、オレにそう言ってた。

Thank you for really listening to me.
But, it seems I wasn't looking for "your answer".
I probably just wanted you to "help me think".

Her eyes, said so to me.

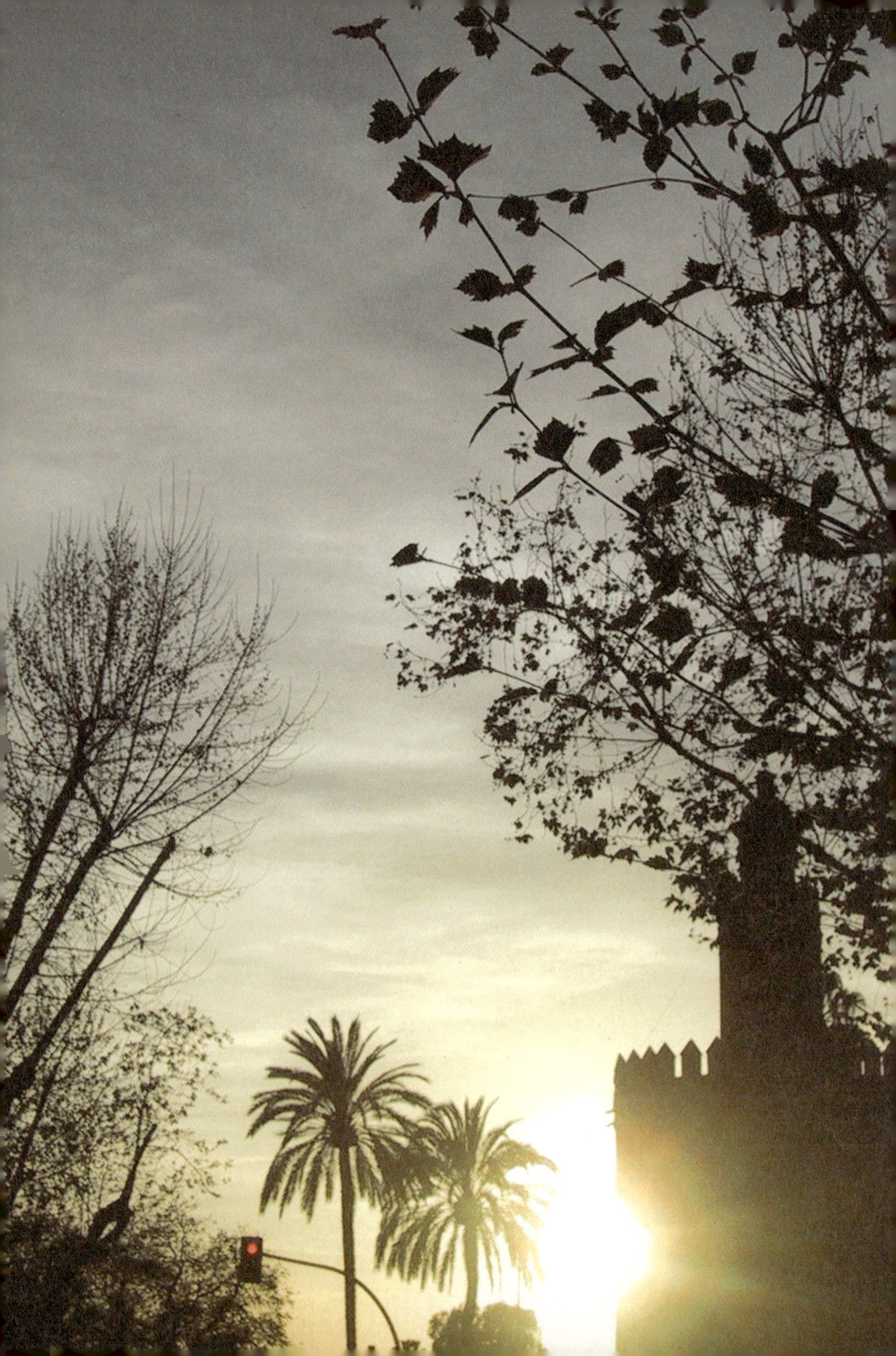

ジブラルタル海峡

ヨーロッパからアフリカへ。
ジブラルタル海峡を越える船の甲板。
ある船乗りのおじさんが言ってた。

「オレは２０年間、世界中をずっとずっと航海してきた。繰り返される日々が嫌いだったからな。でも、愛する女性を見つけた日から、オレは変わった。今は、愛する妻と子供達と一緒に暮らすために、このジブラルタル海峡を１日２往復するだけの繰り返される毎日を過ごしてる。でも、神に誓って言う。今が、一番幸せだ。オレの冒険は、彼女という宝を見つけることで終わったんだ」

そして、キザでかっこいい船乗りは、最後にオレに聞いた。

「オマエは、愛する女性という宝を既に見つけている。いったい、他にどんな宝を探して旅してるんだい？」

Strait of Gibraltar

from Europe to Africa
the deck of the ship crossing the Strait of Gibraltar
some sailor guy said

"For twenty years, I've been sailing all around the world.
Because I hated days of repetition. But from the day
I found the woman I love, I changed. Now, in order to
live with my loving wife and children, my days are
repeated by crossing this Strait of Gibraltar twice a day.
But, I swear to God. I am the happiest now. My adventure
ended when I found her, my treasure."

then finally, the cool, show-off sailor asked me

"You have already found your treasure, the woman you love.
What other treasure could you possibly travel in search of?"

Journey 5 :

Afr

ica

そこのアンタ、
きれいな服を着て、見ているだけかい？

YOU, right there
wearing clean clothes, you just gonna stand and watch?

核

たくさん食べることはない。
一匹の魚を骨まで味わってごらん。
そのほうが、本当の「おいしさ」がわかるから。

たくさん読む必要はない。
一冊の本を文字が溶けるまで味わってごらん。
そのほうが、本当の「おもしろさ」がわかるから。

たくさん愛する必要はない。
ひとりの人を心ゆくまで愛してごらん。
そのほうが、本当の「愛」がわかるから。

貧しい国の豊かな人々が、
オレに、そう笑いかけている。

Core

never eat a lot
one fish, taste it to the bone
you'll understand the real "deliciousness" that way

no need to read a lot
one book, read it until the words melt
you'll understand the real "interest" that way

no need to love a lot
one person, love that person as far as your heart will go
you'll understand real "love" that way

the rich people of poor countries
say so to me, through their smiles

やれば、わかる。

Try it, and you'll see

FOREVER

遂に、きた。
サハラ砂漠だ。

ふたりだけで、ずっとずっと、月明かりの砂漠を歩いた。
ふたりだけで、ずっとずっと、天の川を見ていた。
ふたりだけで、ずっとずっと、風の音を聞いていた。

ノマドと呼ばれる砂漠の民がラクダをひいて歩いている。
どこからともなくジャンベのリズムが聞こえてくる。

なんでこんなにココロが静かなんだろう。

オマエとふたり。
いつも。いつまでも。

Forever

at last, we came
the Sahara Desert

just the two of us, forever and ever
we walked the moonlit desert
just the two of us, forever and ever
we watched the Milky Way
just the two of us, forever and ever
we listened to the sound of the wind

people of the desert called Nomads
pull along camels and walk
from no place in particular
the rhythm of djembes are heard

why is my heart so peaceful?

with YOU, just us
ALWAYS, FOREVER

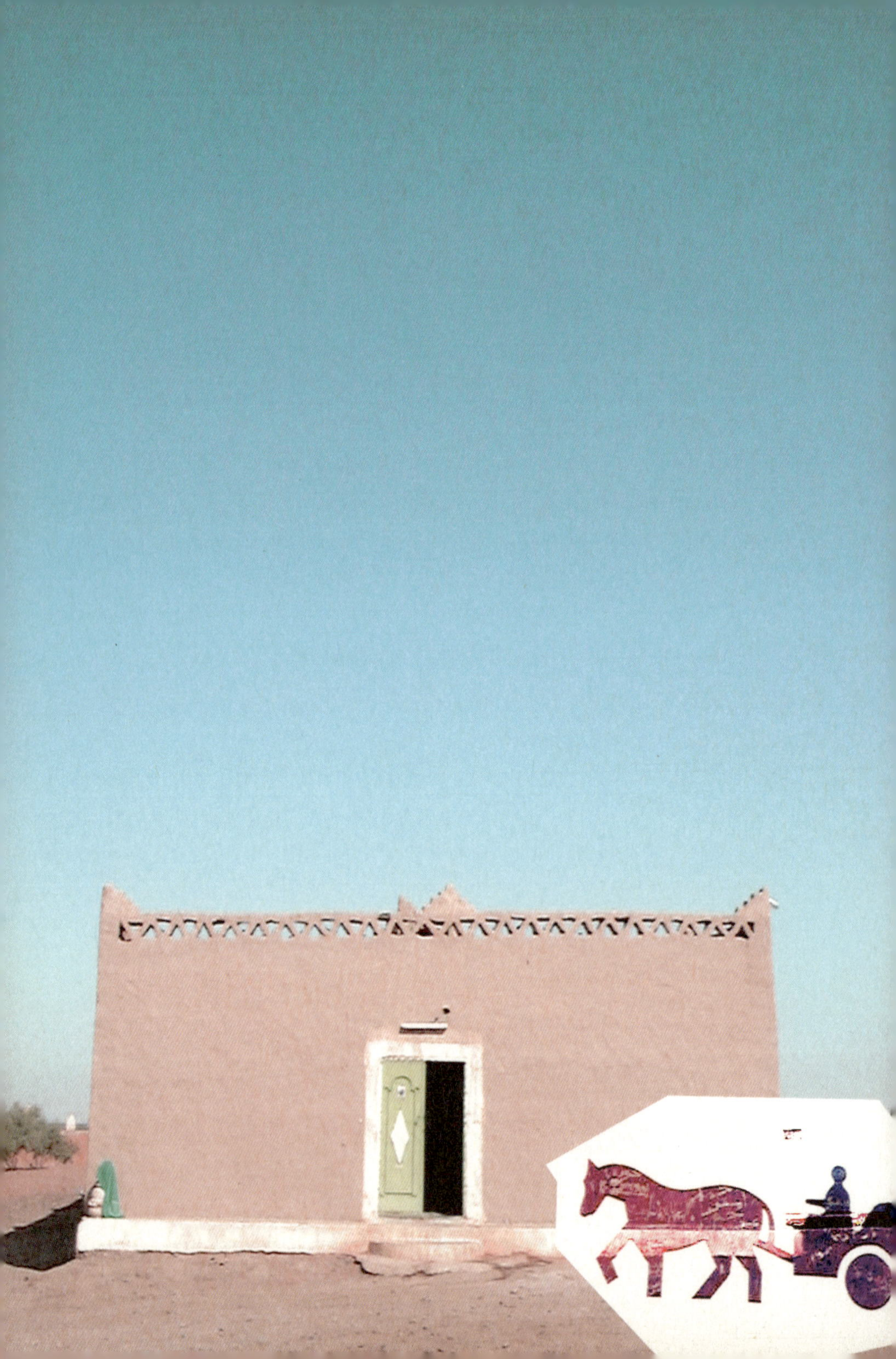

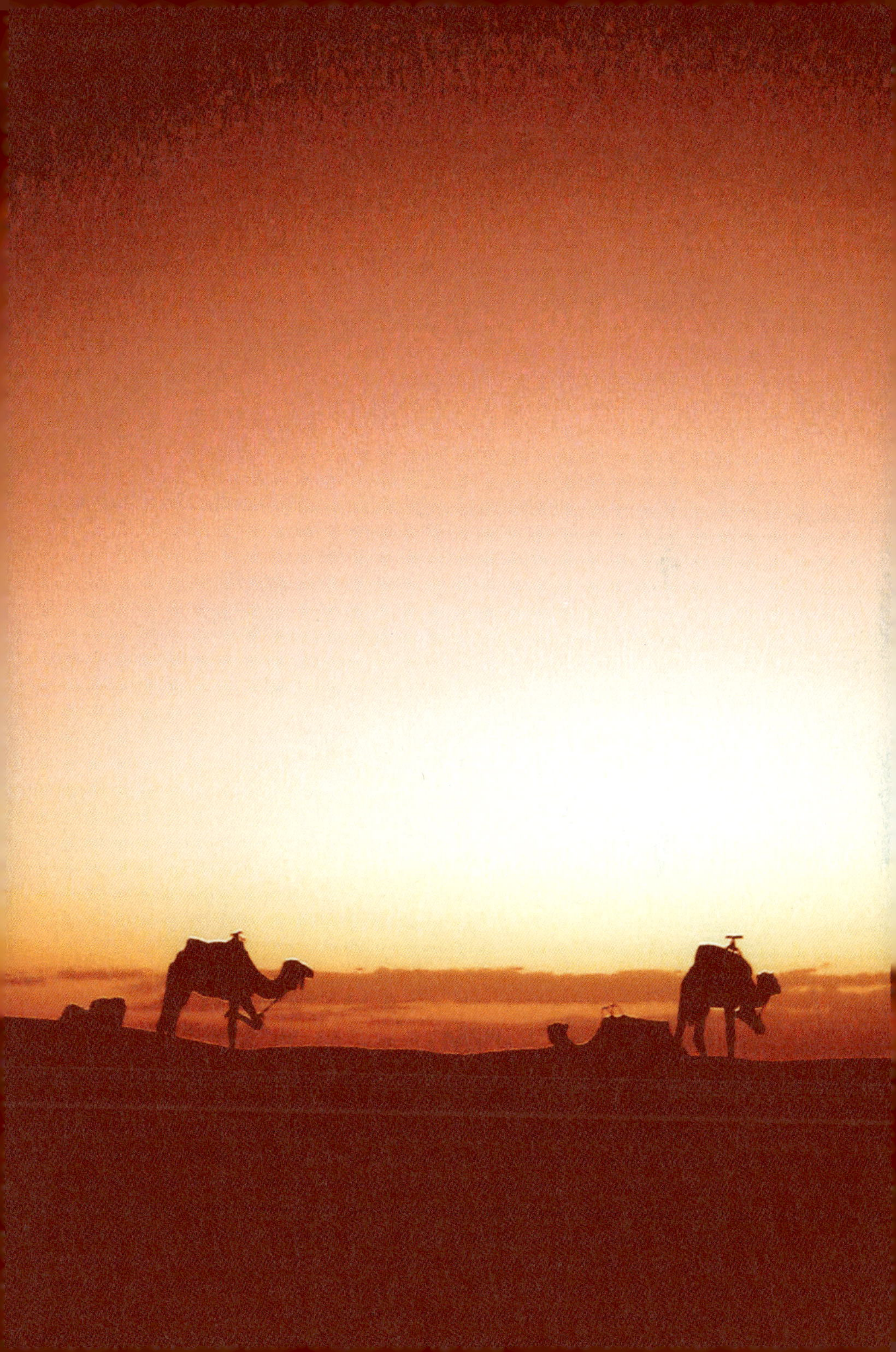

「狭くて、なんでもある場所」にいるときは、
道を選ぶことに必死だった。

「広くて、なんにもない場所」にくると、
ただ歩くだけだった。

選び疲れるよりも、歩き疲れて眠りたい。

when at "a small-enclosed place with everything"
I was desperate to choose a path
come to "a wide-open place with nothing"
I just walked

instead of tiring from choosing
I'd rather tire from walking and go to sleep

未来のために、今を耐えるのではなく、
未来のために、今を楽しく生きるのだ。

For the future, don't bear the present.
For the future, enjoy living the present.

パーフェクト

赤道直下にありながら、雪をたたえて白くそびえるキリマンジャロ。
その麓に広がる野生の王国アンボセリ。

ゾウの群が歩き回り、
茂みからキリンの親子が首を出し、
ハイエナ達が巣でじゃれ回り、
カバが水の中から鼻を出し、
虹をバックに数千羽のピンクフラミンゴが飛び立ち、
その間を真っ赤な布をまとったマサイの人々が歩いている。

この雄大な大地でのラストシーンは、ゾウの出産だった。
大雨の中、泥に足を取られながらも倒れまいと必死に踏ん張っている赤ちゃん。
それを、さりげなく支えてあげている母親。

「すげえ」
ここでは、それ以外のコトバはいらない。

自然のリズムに身体を任せきったとき、
いつもココロの中から全身に広がっていく、
この「透明な感情」はなんなんだろう？
この感情の中に、オレの探しているパーフェクトは、きっとある。

Perfect

Although directly below the equator, whitely patted
with snow towers Mt. Kilimanjaro.
At the foot of that spreads a kingdom of the wild,
Amboseli.

Elephants walking around in herds
Giraffes poking their necks out of bushes
Hyenas playing around in their nest
Hippos poking their noses out of the water
with a rainbow in the background, a few thousand Pink
Flamingos flying away
In the middle of all that, people of the Masai Tribe,
wrapped in red cloth, are walking.

The last scene in this grand land of nature, was the
birth of an elephant.
In the pouring rain, desperately trying not to fall,
losing his footing in the mud, was a newborn elephant.
And, nonchalantly supporting it, was its mother.

"Amazing"
Here, no other words are needed.

When entrusting my entire body to the rhythm of nature,
What is this "clear emotion" that always spreads from
inside the heart to the entire body?
Within this emotion probably lies the PERFECTION I am
searching for.

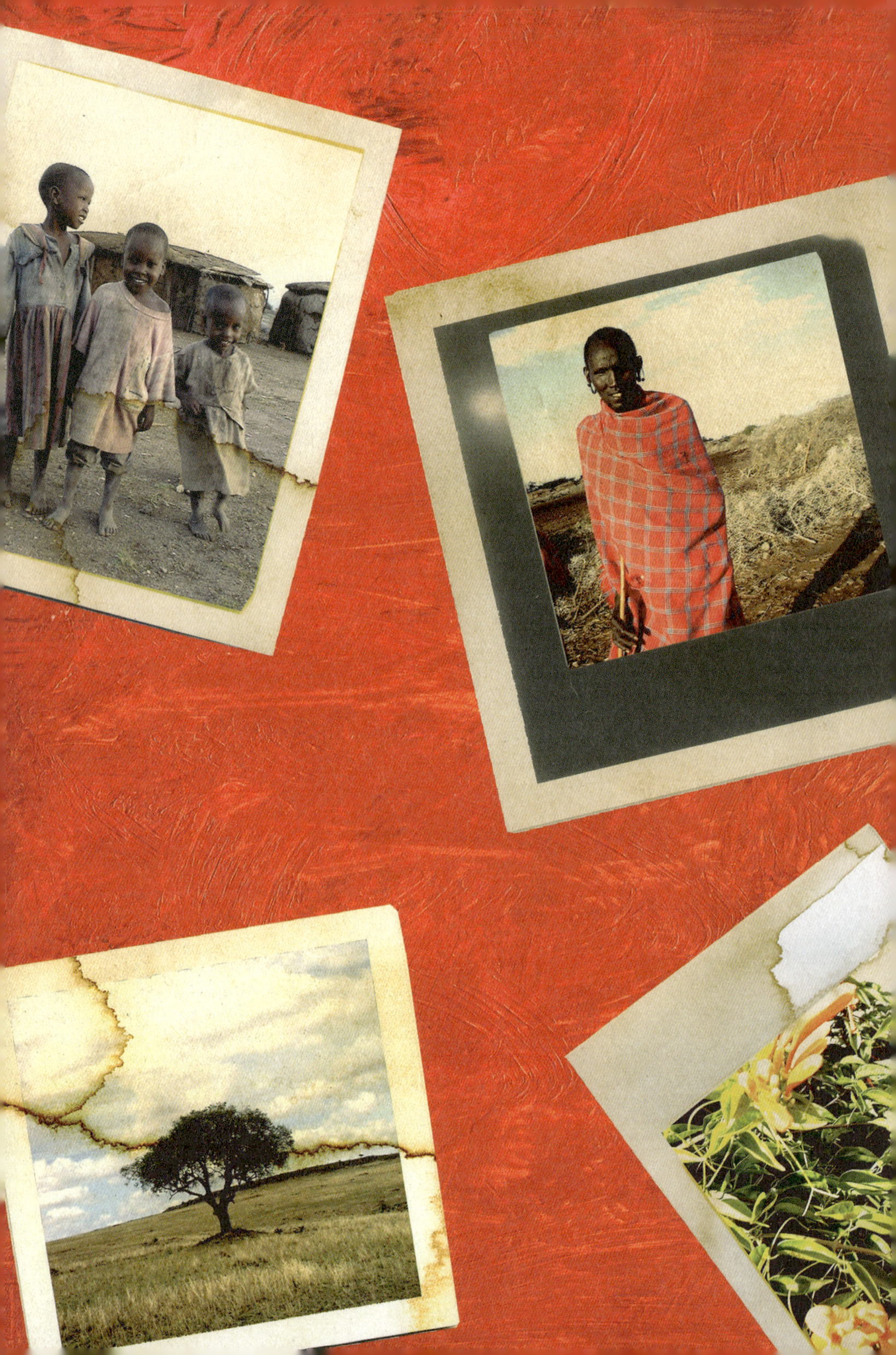

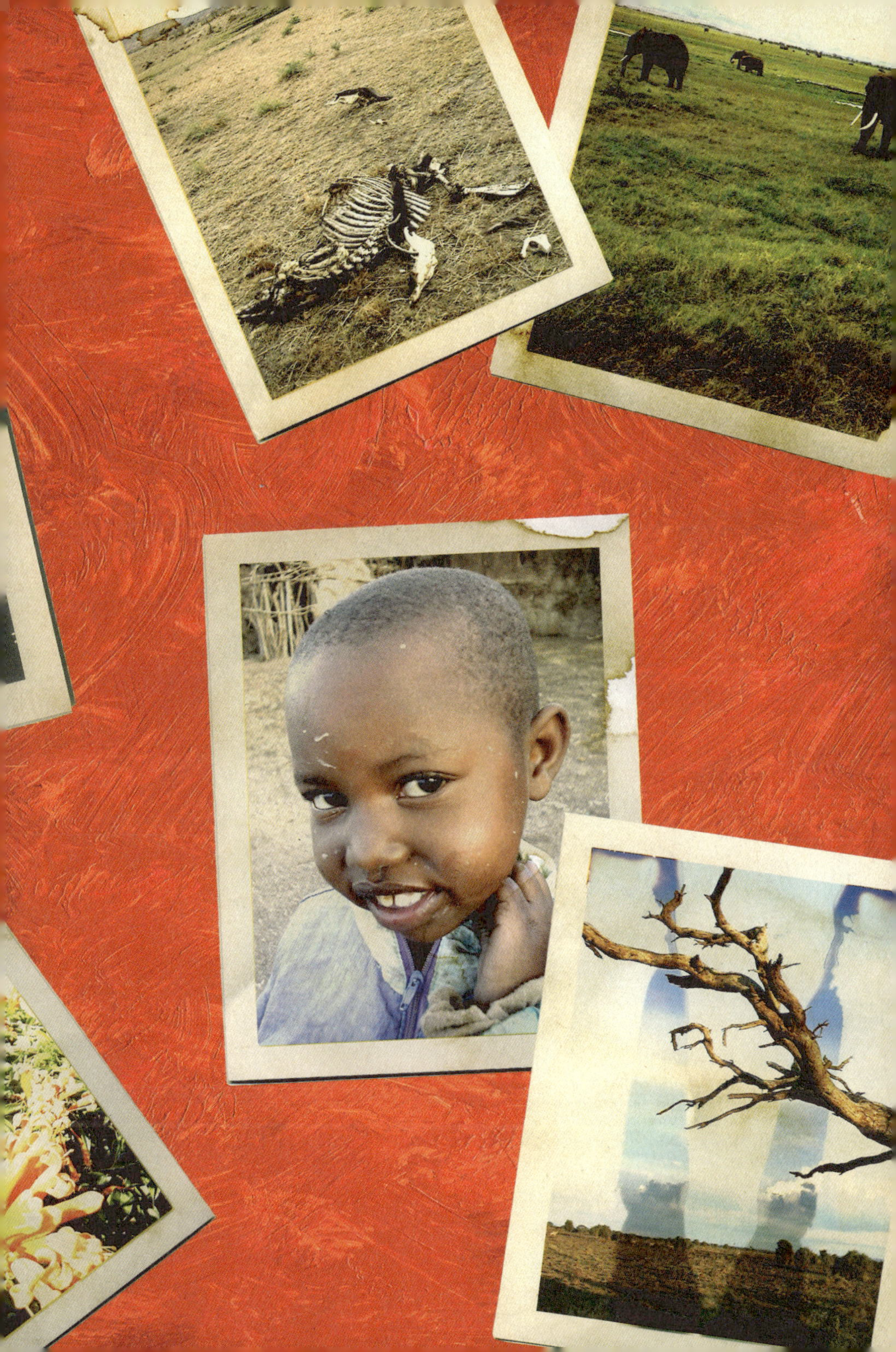

本当に大切なもの以外、すべて捨ててしまえばいいのに。

Except for what's really important,
we should throw away everything else.

もっと肌で。もっと身体で。

More through the skin.   More through the entire body.

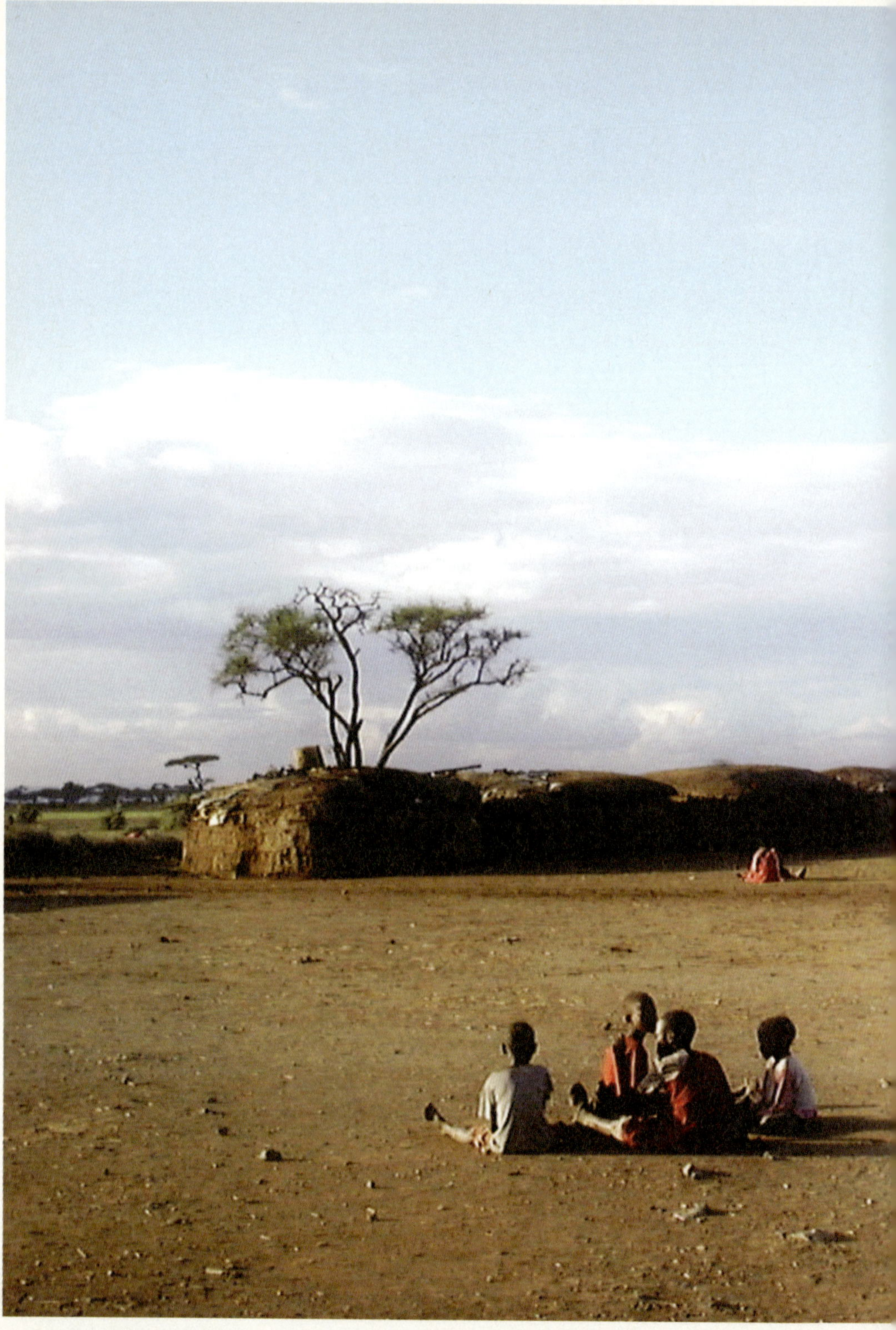

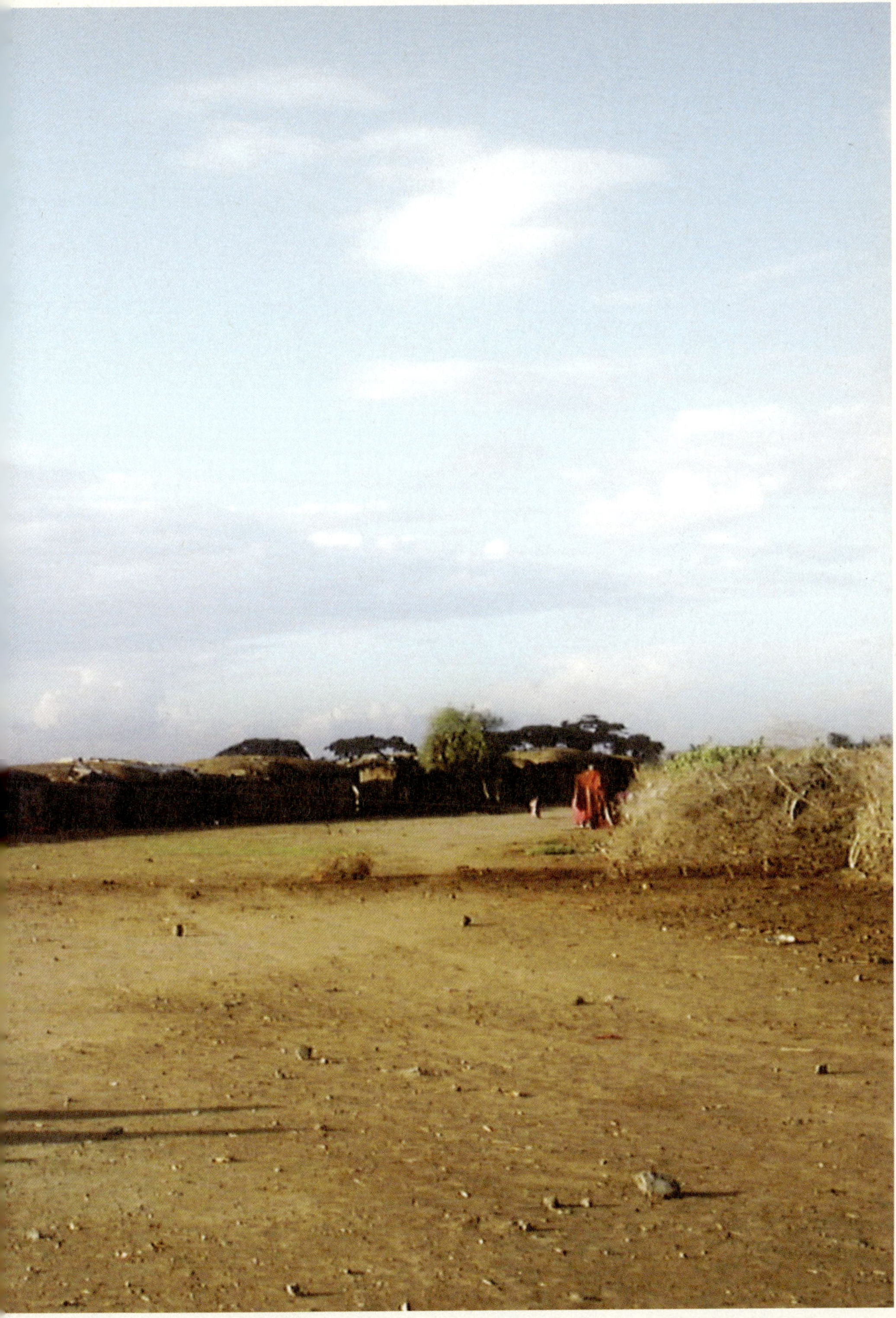

自分らしさ？

「自分らしい生き方？」「ナチュラルな生き方？」
そんなの自分自身でわかるわけないじゃん！

それぞれ、みんな。
ただ、毎日の暮らしの中で、
「自分が美しいと思う行い」を積み重ねていけばいいさ。

My Way?

"My way of life?" "A natural way of life?"
No way you can know that on your own!

Everyone, respectively.
Just, in everyday life,
An accumulation of "doing what you think is beautiful"
is just fine.

One Love

ケニア。赤道直下の路上マーケットで。
アフリカンガールのルーシーが石に刻んでくれた
3つの小さなコトバたち。

ONE LOVE.
ONE SOUL.
ONE HEART.

そんな想いでずっといられたら、
きっとオレタチはつながっていられる。

One Love

Kenya, at a street market directly below the equator
Lucy, an African girl, carved 3 short phrases into a rock

ONE LOVE
ONE SOUL
ONE HEART

If we can always keep that in mind
We can probably be connected

アナタは人生に、なにを望んでいるの？

What do YOU want in life?

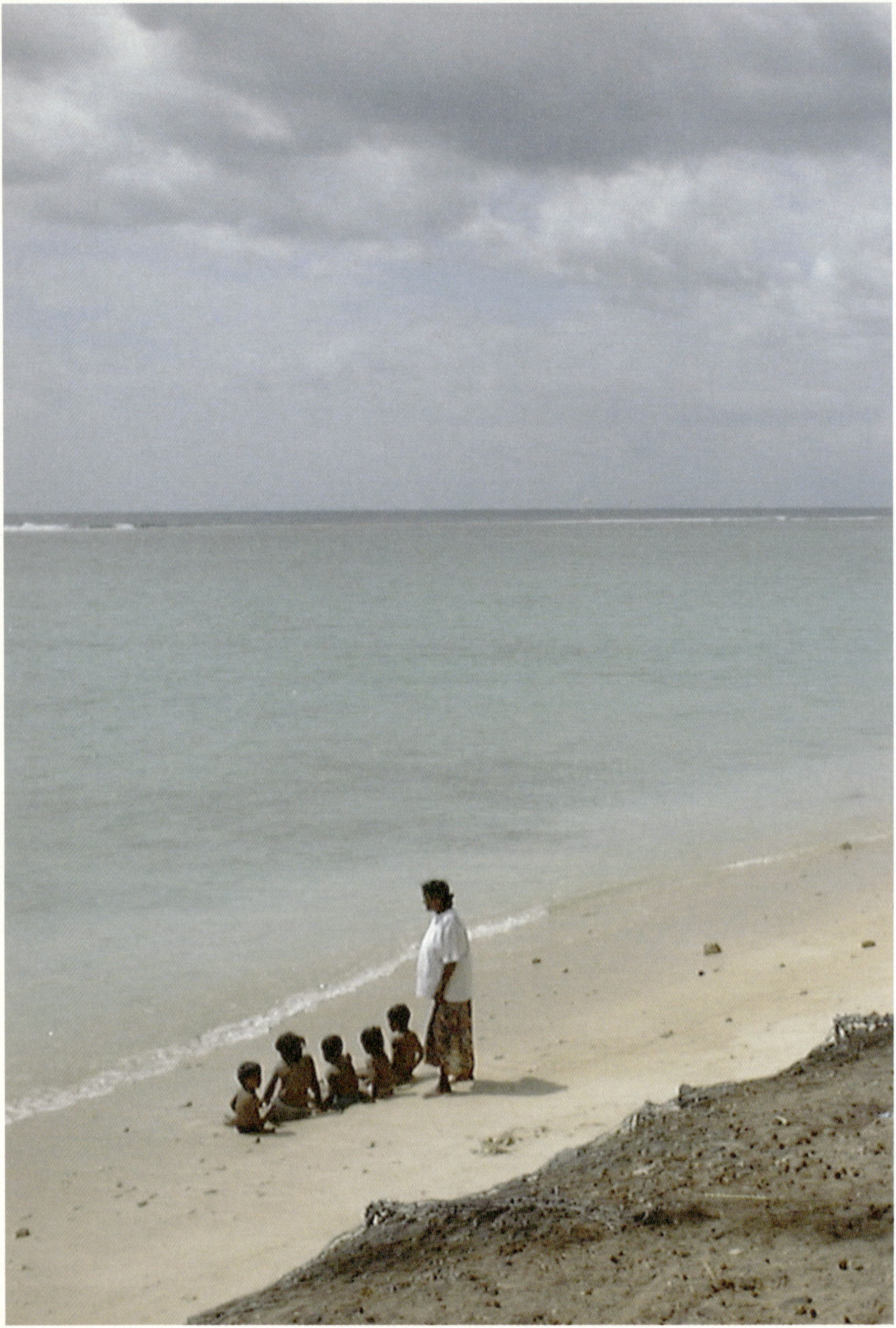

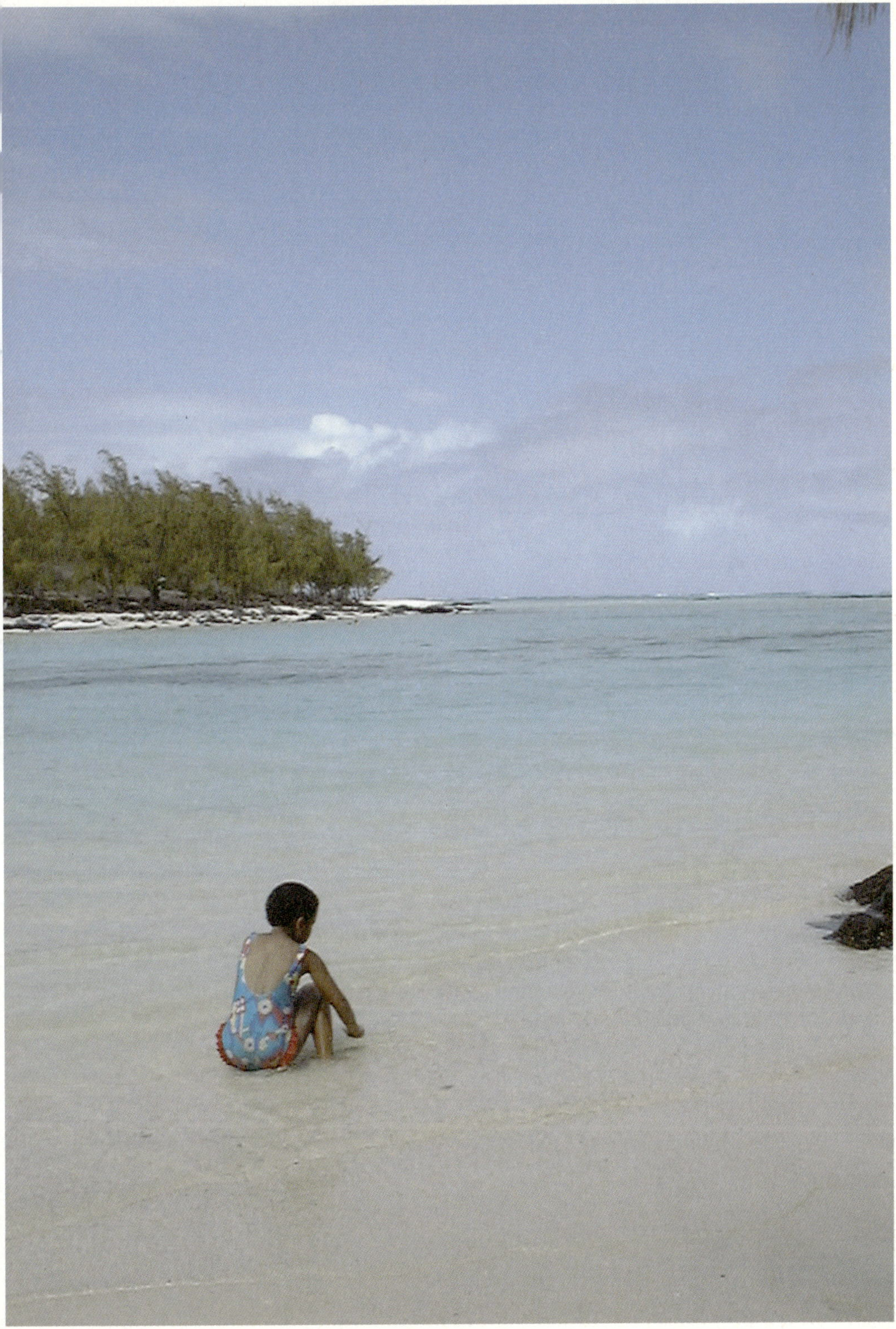

Journey 6 :

South & North A

merica

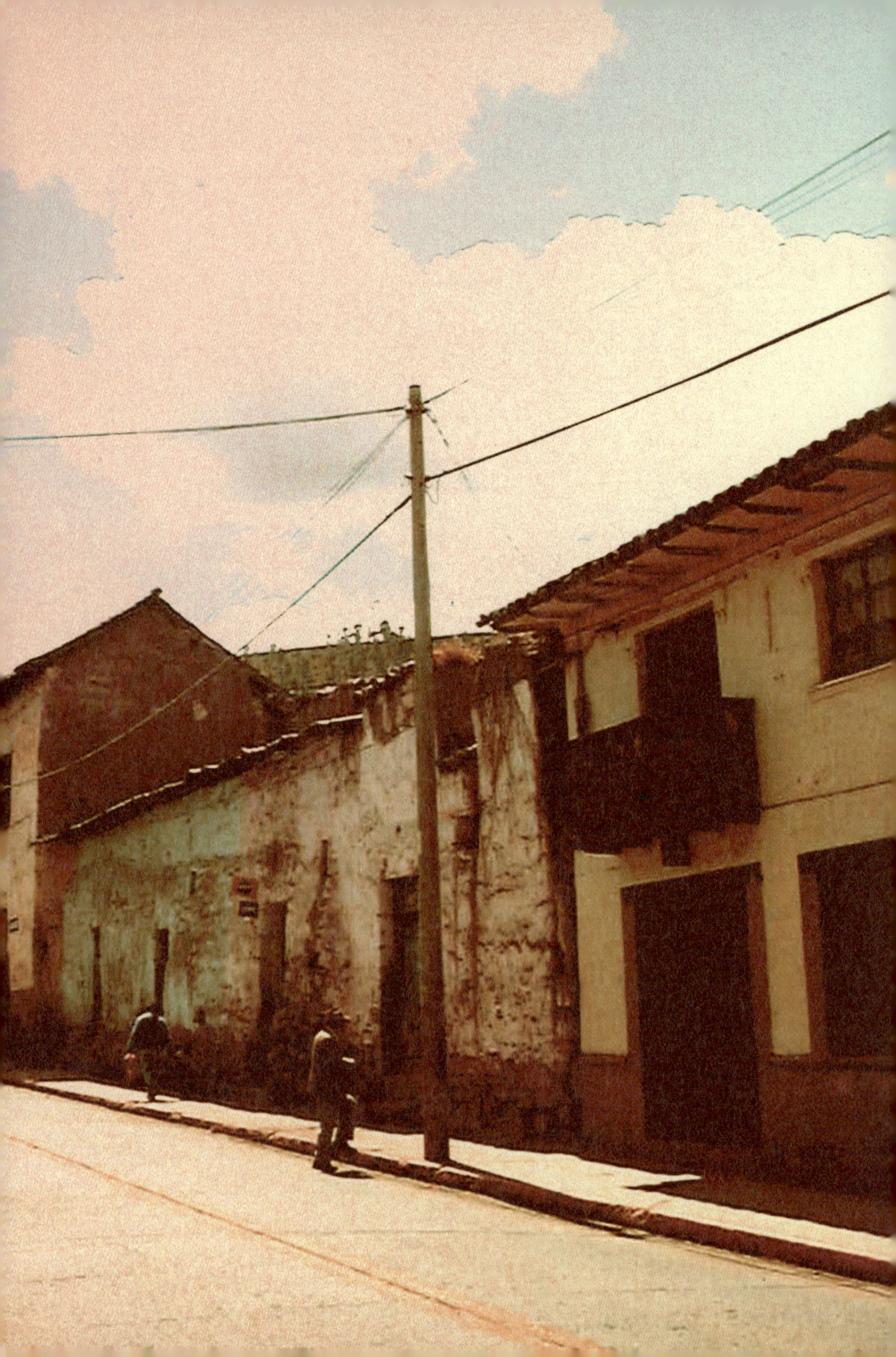

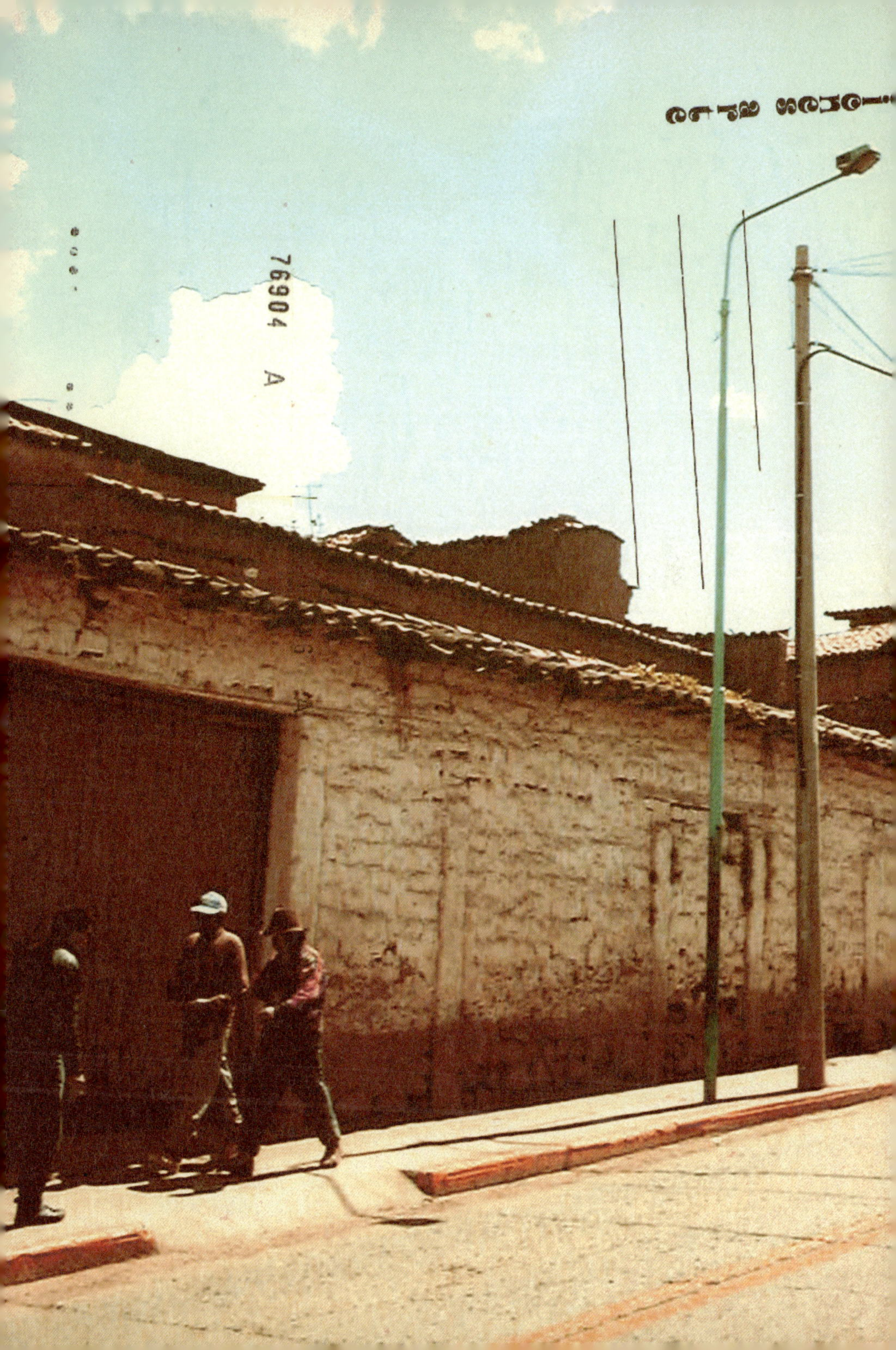

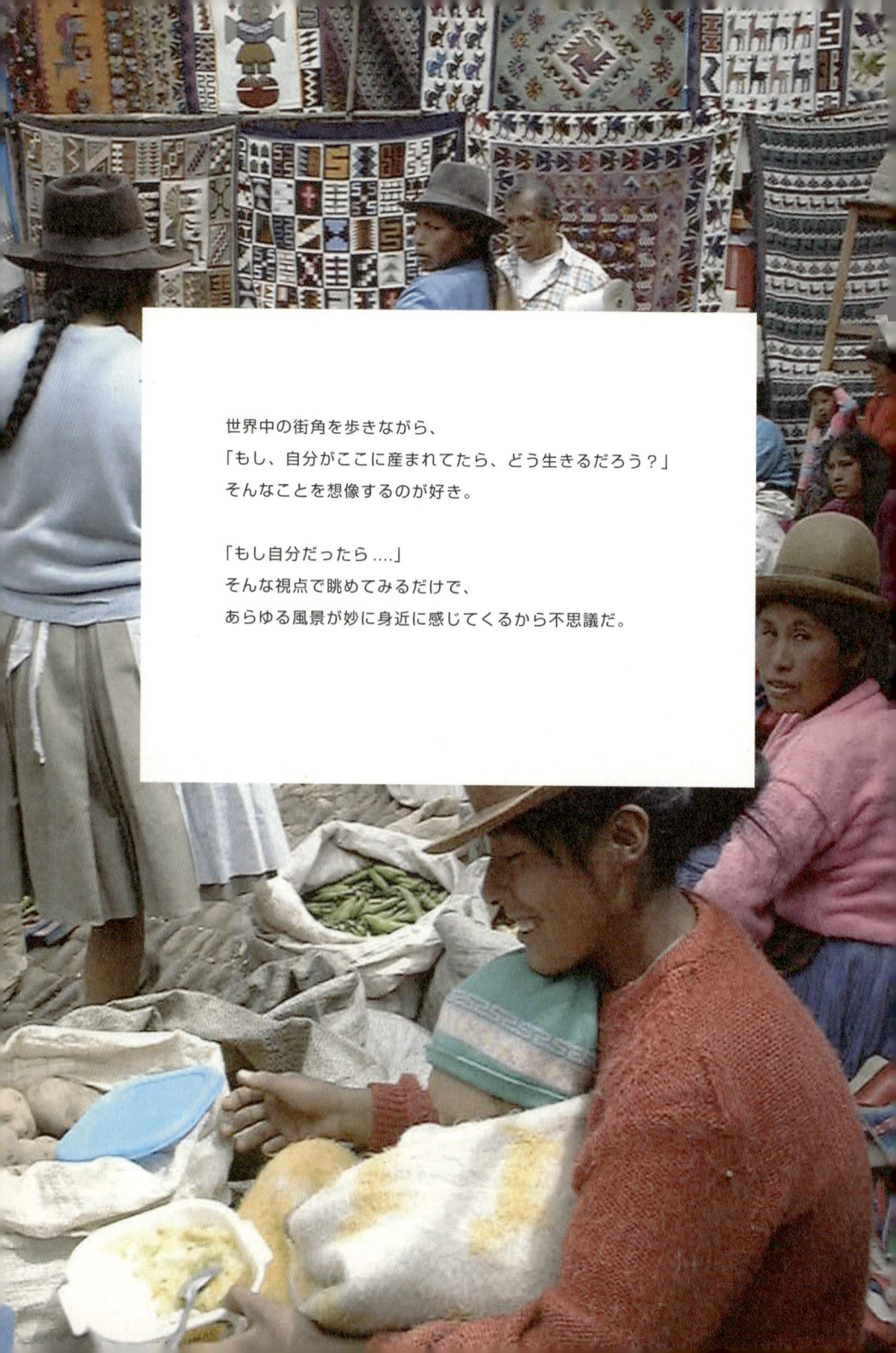

世界中の街角を歩きながら、
「もし、自分がここに産まれてたら、どう生きるだろう？」
そんなことを想像するのが好き。

「もし自分だったら....」
そんな視点で眺めてみるだけで、
あらゆる風景が妙に身近に感じてくるから不思議だ。

walking the street corners of the world
"if I was born here, how would I be living?"
I like to imagine such things

"if that were me..."
just seeing things from that point of view
strange how, every possible scenery somehow starts
to feel closer to me

ただの「HOTな虫けら」でいたい。
ずっと。

I just wanna be a "HOT little bug"
Always

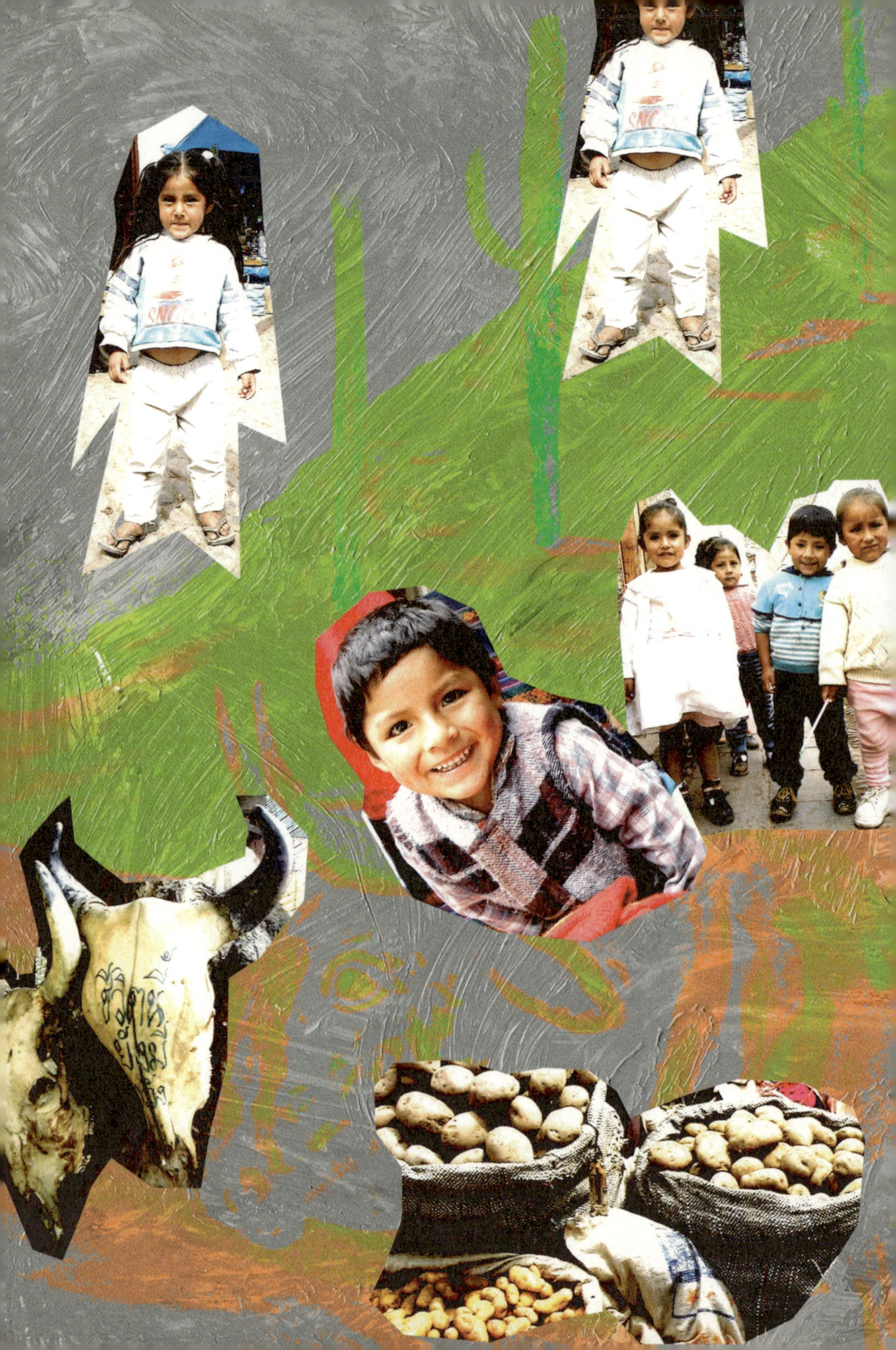

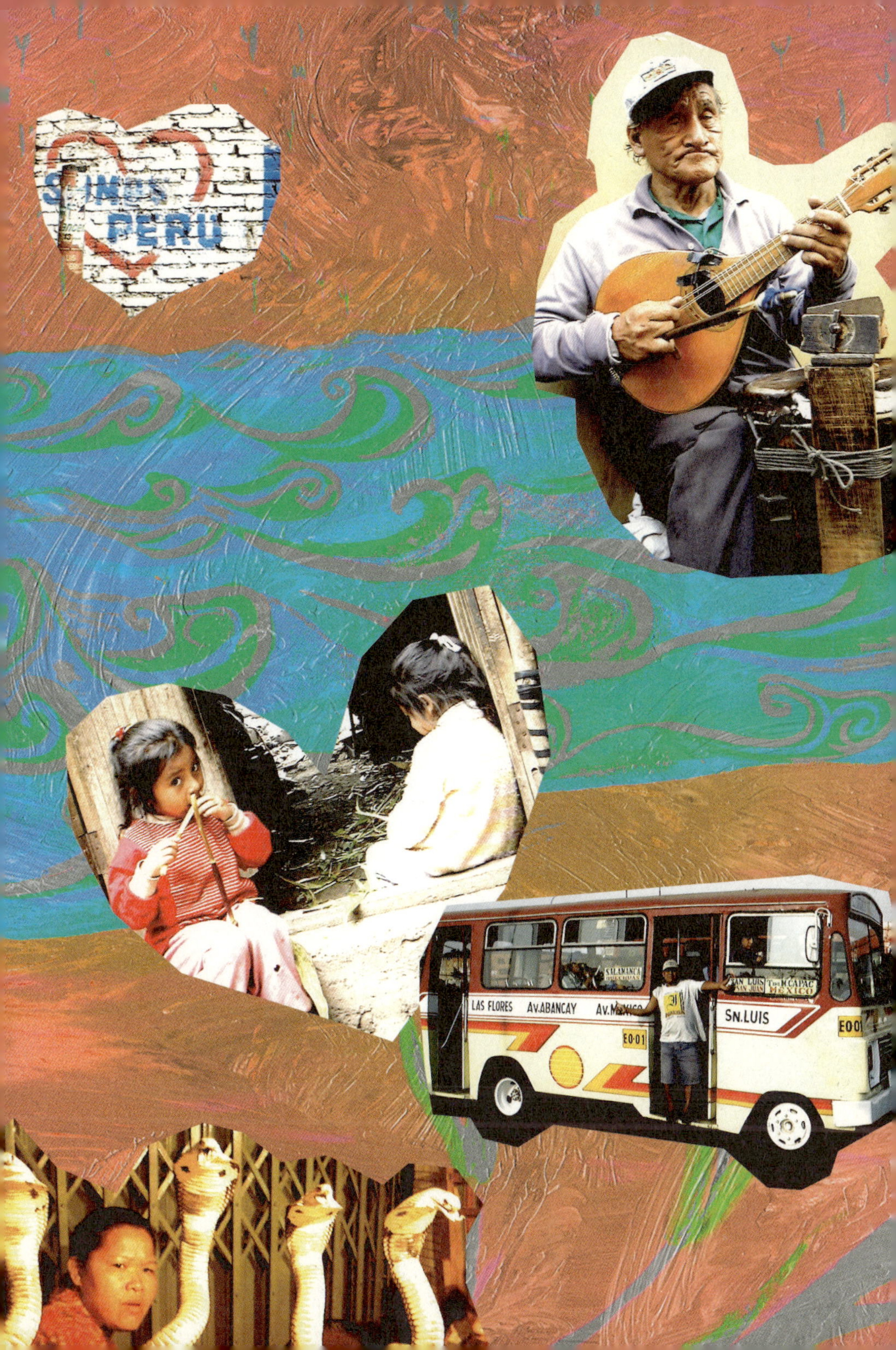
PERU
LAS FLORES
Av.ABANCAY
SN.LUIS

ヒントはあるが、ルールはない

いろいろな生き方に触れれば触れるほど、
「こんな生き方もありなんだ」って、自分の選択肢も広がる。

いろいろな価値観に触れれば触れるほど、
「じゃ、自分はどうなんだ？」って、自分の価値観を確かめることになる。

他人を知るということは、
自分を知るということでもある。

There are Hints, but No Rules

The more and more lifestyles I come in contact with
"This lifestyle works, too" I'll think
And my options will expand

The more and more sense of values I come in contact with
"OK, how about me?" I'll think
And I'll reconfirm my own sense of values

To know others is
to also know yourself

オレの中で、
日々変わっていくことがある。
そして、決して変わらないことがある。

サヤカの中にも、
日々変わっていくことがある。
そして、決して変わらないことがある。

互いの中にある「決して変わらない部分」を愛おしいと思えたから、
きっと、オレタチは一緒にいるんだろう。

within me
there are things that change everyday
and, there are things that never change

within Sayaka, too
there are things that change everyday
and, there are things that never change

because we both cherish each other's
"things that never change"
I'm sure, that's why WE are together

アイランドトリップ

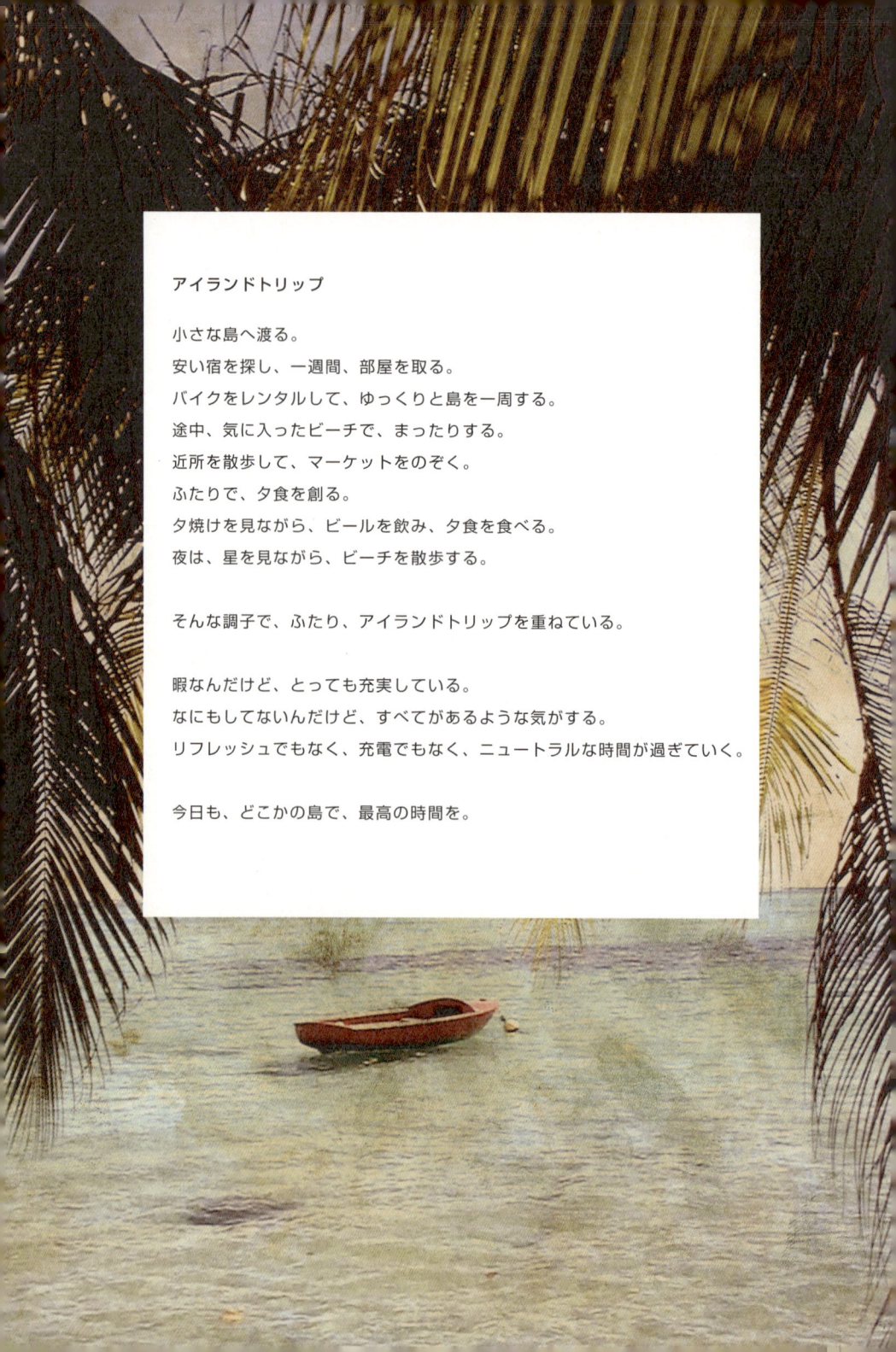

小さな島へ渡る。
安い宿を探し、一週間、部屋を取る。
バイクをレンタルして、ゆっくりと島を一周する。
途中、気に入ったビーチで、まったりする。
近所を散歩して、マーケットをのぞく。
ふたりで、夕食を創る。
夕焼けを見ながら、ビールを飲み、夕食を食べる。
夜は、星を見ながら、ビーチを散歩する。

そんな調子で、ふたり、アイランドトリップを重ねている。

暇なんだけど、とっても充実している。
なにもしてないんだけど、すべてがあるような気がする。
リフレッシュでもなく、充電でもなく、ニュートラルな時間が過ぎていく。

今日も、どこかの島で、最高の時間を。

Island Trip

crossing over to a small island
we find a cheap hotel room
and get a room for a week
we rent a motorbike
and take a slow ride around the island
somewhere in between
we find a beach we like, and relax
we take a walk in the area
and peek into the market
together, we make dinner
while watching the sun set
we drink beer, and eat dinner
at night, watching the stars
we take a walk on the beach

in that way, the two of us, are repeating
island trips

we have time to spare, but it is very enriching
not doing anything, but feeling as if we have
everything
not refreshing, not recharging, but neutral
time passing

and again today, on some island
we'll have a peaceful time

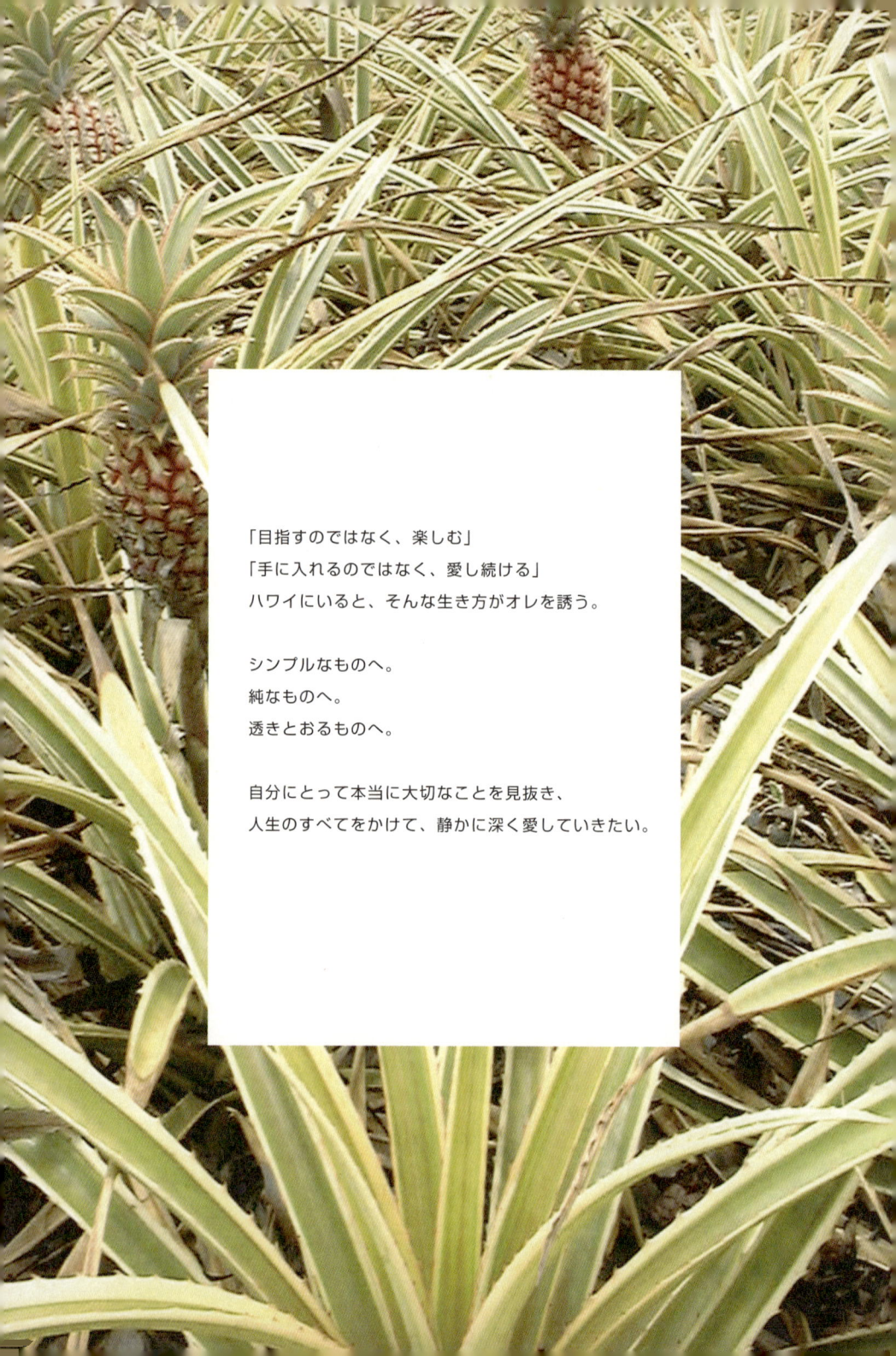

「目指すのではなく、楽しむ」
「手に入れるのではなく、愛し続ける」
ハワイにいると、そんな生き方がオレを誘う。

シンプルなものへ。
純なものへ。
透きとおるものへ。

自分にとって本当に大切なことを見抜き、
人生のすべてをかけて、静かに深く愛していきたい。

"not to aim for, but to have fun"
"not to own, but to keep loving"
being in Hawaii, that kind of life invites me

towards something simple
towards something pure
towards something transparent

having insight to what is really important to me
I want to spend a lifetime, quietly, deeply loving

「自分の魂が本当に満たされるっていうのは、どういうことなのでしょうか？」

「それはね、自分が本当に何をしたいのか、何をするためにこの世に生を受けたのかを知ることです。いくらお金があっても、いい仕事を持っていても、自分の魂を満足させられないと、病気になったり、悪いことを引き起こしたりしてしまいます。いろいろな辛い経験を踏み、苦しい体験を経てこそ、その中から自分にとっての本当の幸せを学び取るものなのです」
「だから、本当に必要なものを見つけるまで、魂は旅を続けます。ただじっと待っていても幸せにはなれません。また不必要な物を捨て去ることができなければ、新しく得ることもできません。変化をする時はいつも大変ですが、不必要な物を捨て去る決断を下せない人の魂は決して満たされることがないでしょう」

〜あるハワイアンの言葉より〜

"What Does it Mean to Truly Satisfy One's Soul?"

"That is, to know what you really want to do, what you came to do in this world. No matter how much money you have, or how good a job you have; if you don't satisfy your soul, you can become ill, or bad things can happen to you. Experience various hardships and pain, and from that you will learn what is true happiness."
"That is why the soul will continue the journey, until it finds what is really necessary. Standing still and waiting will not bring happiness. And if you cannot rid of unnecessary things, you cannot acquire anything new. Times of change are always difficult, but those who cannot make the decision to rid themselves of those unnecessary things, their souls will never be satisfied."

-- words of an Anonymous Hawaiian --

雨が降るから、虹もでる

〜虹の州・ハワイの標語より〜

No Rain, No Rainbow
It rains; therefore, there are rainbows.

- The Rainbow State, Hawaiian saying -

BELIEVE YOUR トリハダ
鳥肌は嘘をつかない。

Believe Your Goosebumps
Goosebumps don't lie

世界中の国に「国旗」があるように、
それぞれの人に「人旗」（ジンキ!?）があったらおもしろいのにね。

アナタなら、どんな旗を掲げて生きる？

Like all countries of the world have a "national flag"
Wouldn't it be interesting if everyone had a
"personal flag"?

What kind of flag would you raise to live by?

アラスカ

極北の地、アラスカ。
ここが、今回の世界大冒険の最終地点になる。

何千匹というサーモンの群が、川をのぼり、卵を産み、死んでいくのを見ていた。
母熊が子熊に、命がけで狩りを教えるのを見ていた。
何万年もかけて創られた氷河が、爆音とともに崩れ落ちていくのを見ていた。
朽ち果てた倒木を養分にして、成長していこうとする新しい芽を見ていた。
どこまでもどこまでも続く、人類未踏の荒野を見ていた。
大雨が降り、新しい川が生まれるのを見ていた。

オレは、いつも、「こっそり」見ていた。
オレは、いつも、「だまって」見ていた。

大きなものに出逢い、自分の小ささを痛いほどに感じながら。
大きなものに出逢い、自分の可能性を震えるほどに感じながら。

Alaska

Land of the far north, Alaska
This will be the last stop on this great world adventure

I watched thousands of schools of salmon, swim up-river,
lay eggs, and die
I watched a mother bear, risking death, to teach her
cub how to hunt
I watched a glacier, formed through tens of thousands
of years crumbling with an explosion
I watched a new bud, striving to grow through the
nourishment of a rotting tree trunk
I watched a wilderness, never trodden by man, that
countries forever and ever
I watched a new river, forming after a rainstorm

I always watched "secretly"
I always watched "silently"

I encountered big things, feeling my smallness, painfully.
I encountered big things, feeling my potential, trembling.

ハッピーに生きていくために、一番大切なこと。
それは、きっと、自分を知るということ。

In order to live happily, the most important thing
Surely, that is to know oneself

自分を知るためには、
自分と話せばいい。

自分と話すためには、
まず、自分に質問してみればいい。

ゆっくり、ゆっくりと。
すべての答えは、必ず、自分の中にあるから。

to get to know yourself
speak to yourself

to speak to yourself
first, ask yourself questions

slowly, slowly
all the answers, difinitely, are inside of you

カリキュラム

今、自分に起こっている現実は、すべて、「神様の仕組んだカリキュラム」。
現実を「ポジティブ」にとらえるのではなく、
現実を「ネガティブ」にとらえるのでもなく、
ただ、今、自分が学ぶべきことを見極め、きっちりと学んでいけばいいのさ。

Curriculum

Everything that is happening to me now in reality is a "curriculum planned by God"
Not to capture reality as "positive"
Not to capture reality as "negative"
Just pick up on what you're supposed to be learning now, and study it properly

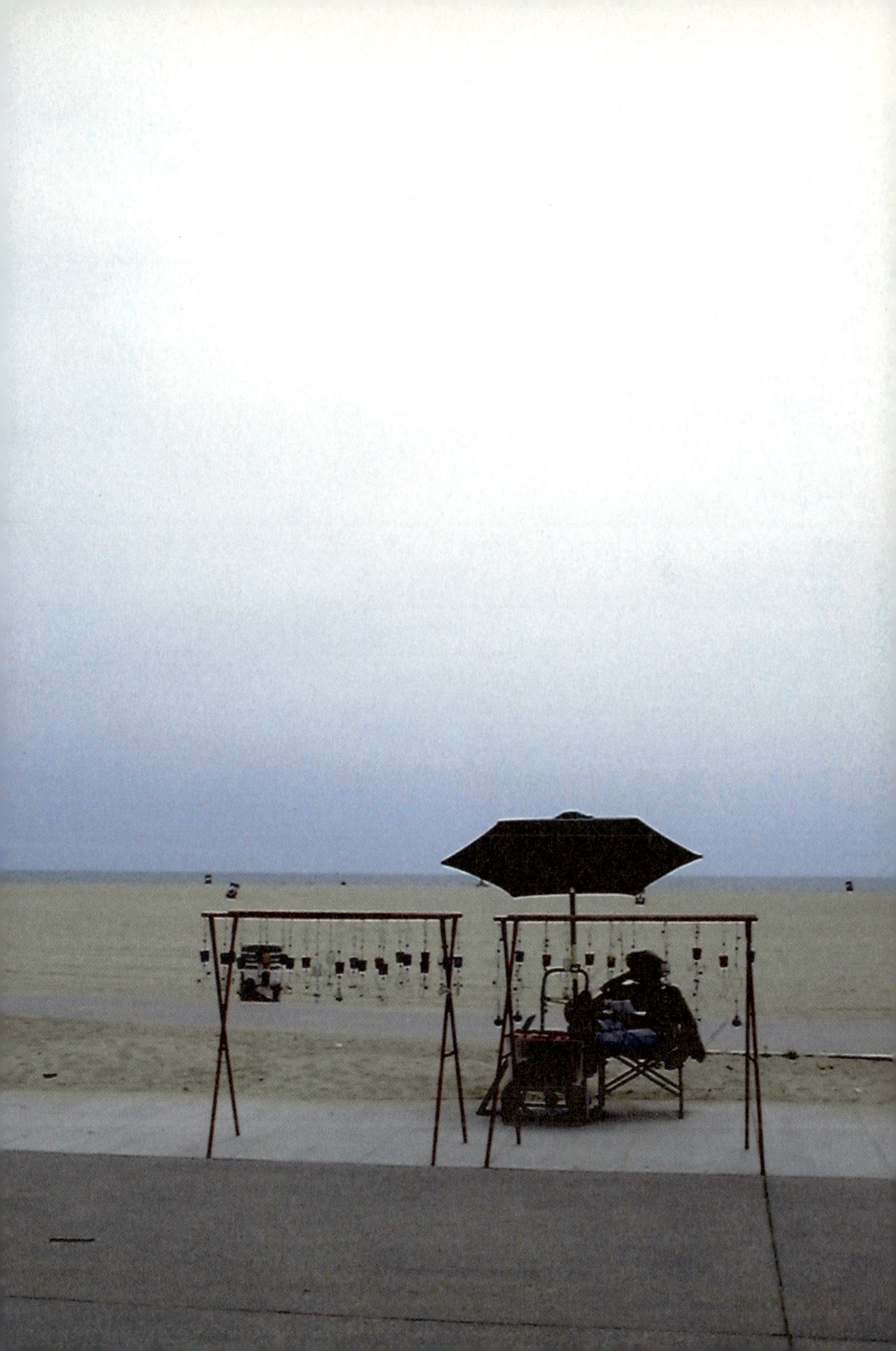

必要なのは、勇気ではなく、覚悟。
決めてしまえば、すべては動き始める。

What is necessary is not courage, but determination.
Make a decision, and all the wheels will begin rolling.

「きっと、この場面は一生忘れないだろうな....」
さやかとふたりで、そんな時間をいっぱい分けあえたこと。

それだけで、この旅は、じゅうぶんだったな。

さやかの求めている「幸せのカタチ」
オレの求めている「幸せのカタチ」
それを伝えあえたこと。
そして、大半の部分を共有できる自信を得られたこと。

それだけで、この旅は、じゅうぶんだったな。

"I will never forget this scene..."
Sayaka and I shared so many, many times like this

Just that, was enough to make this journey worthwhile

"The form of Happiness" that Sayaka seeks
"The form of Happiness" that I seek
That we were able to convey to each other
and the confidence that we both gained from knowing
we share most of them

Just that, was enough to make this journey worthwhile

あなたにとって、本当に大切な人は誰ですか？
あなたにとって、本当に大切なことは何ですか？

Who is the most important person to you?
What is the most important thing to you?

YOU
おまえがいるから。

YOU
because you are here

大切なことに気づく場所は、いつも、
パソコンの前ではなく、青空の下だった。

the place I realized important things was always
not in front of a computer, but under a blue sky

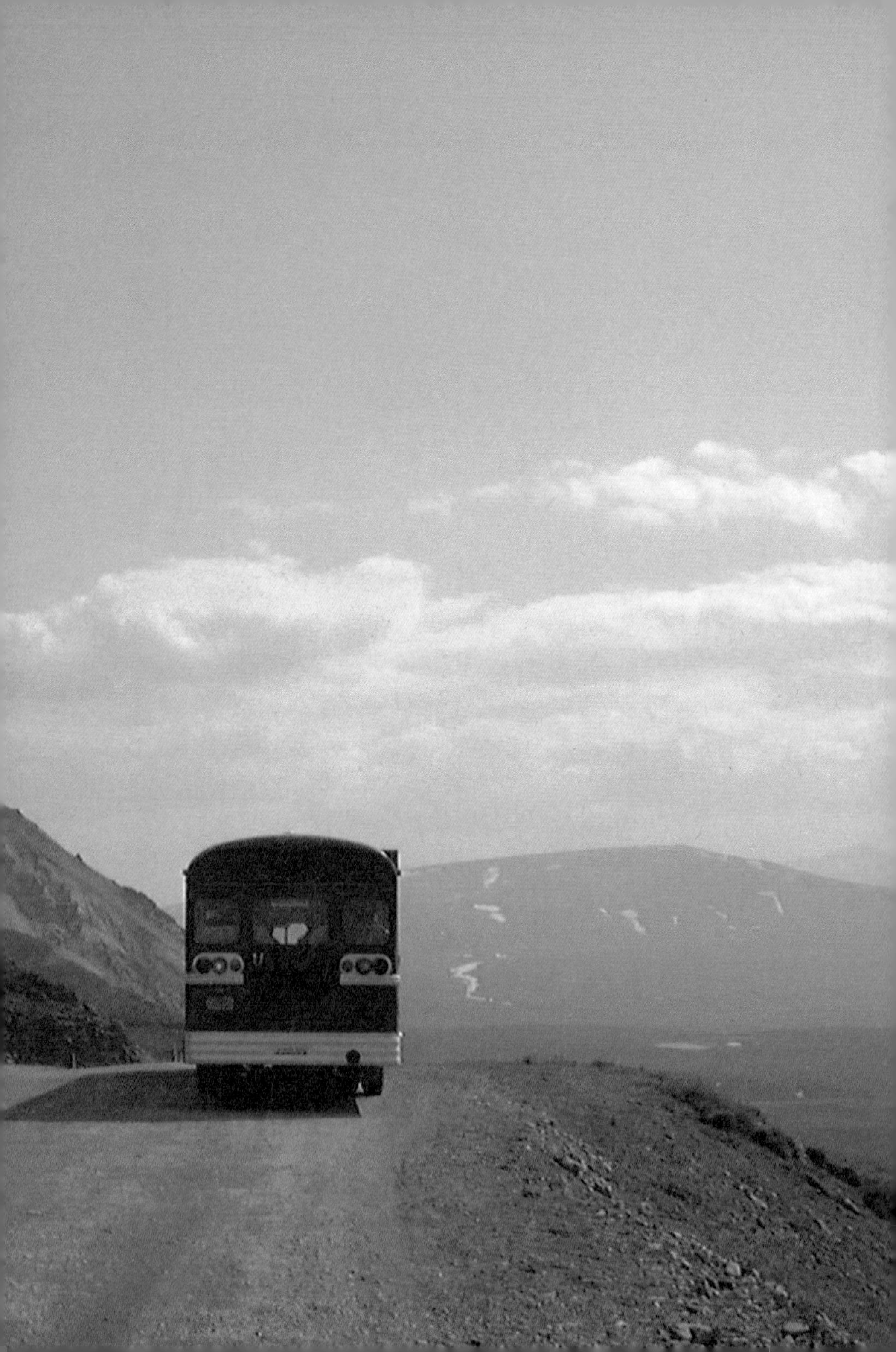

Journey Final :

J a p

a

夕陽に感動する余裕を持って、毎日を生きよう。
夕陽は、いつもそこにある。

Let's live everyday, with enough room in our hearts
to be touched by the sunset.
The sunset, is always, right there.

FACE

日本に帰ってきてから、1ヶ月が過ぎた。
最近のオレは、なんだか、そわそわしている気がする。

なぜだかわからないけど、やることがたくさんあり、
なにかをしている実感がないままに、あっという間に時間が過ぎていく。

旅中、毎日書いていた日記も、知らぬ間につけなくなった。
旅中、毎日言葉を刻んでいたノートも、手につかなくなった。
なんだか、「自分のココロの井戸を掘り下げていく作業」を、面倒に感じるようになっている。

それなりの居心地のよさと、それなりの安心感に包まれ、
生きていくうえでの、緊張感のようなものが、少々欠けてしまっているような気がする。

日本という国の時間の流れの中で、
自分の道をきちんと歩きつづけるためには、
「自分と向き合う時間」を意識的に創っていく必要があるな。

Face

It's been a month since returning to Japan.
Lately, for some reason, I feel like I'm restless.

I don't know why, but there is so much to do.
Not really registering that I am doing something,
but time flies by.

The journal I kept everyday during my journey,
without realizing, I've quit writing in.
The notebook I recorded phrases in everyday during
my journey, I haven't touched.
Somehow, "the process of digging into the bottom of
my heart's well" has started to become a chore.

Feeling somewhat comfortable, and surrounded by
some amount of security,
I feel like I've started to lose the tension in life,
little by little.

In the time that flows through this country, Japan,
To be sure to keep walking along my own path,
I feel the need to consciously make "time to face
myself".

誰かを愛するということは、
誰かを愛さないということ。

何かを選ぶということは、
何かを捨てるということ。

俺は、捨てる勇気が、まだ足りないみたいだ。

To love someone means
Not to love someone

To choose something means
To abandon something

It looks like, I still lack the courage to abandon.

銀河
両関

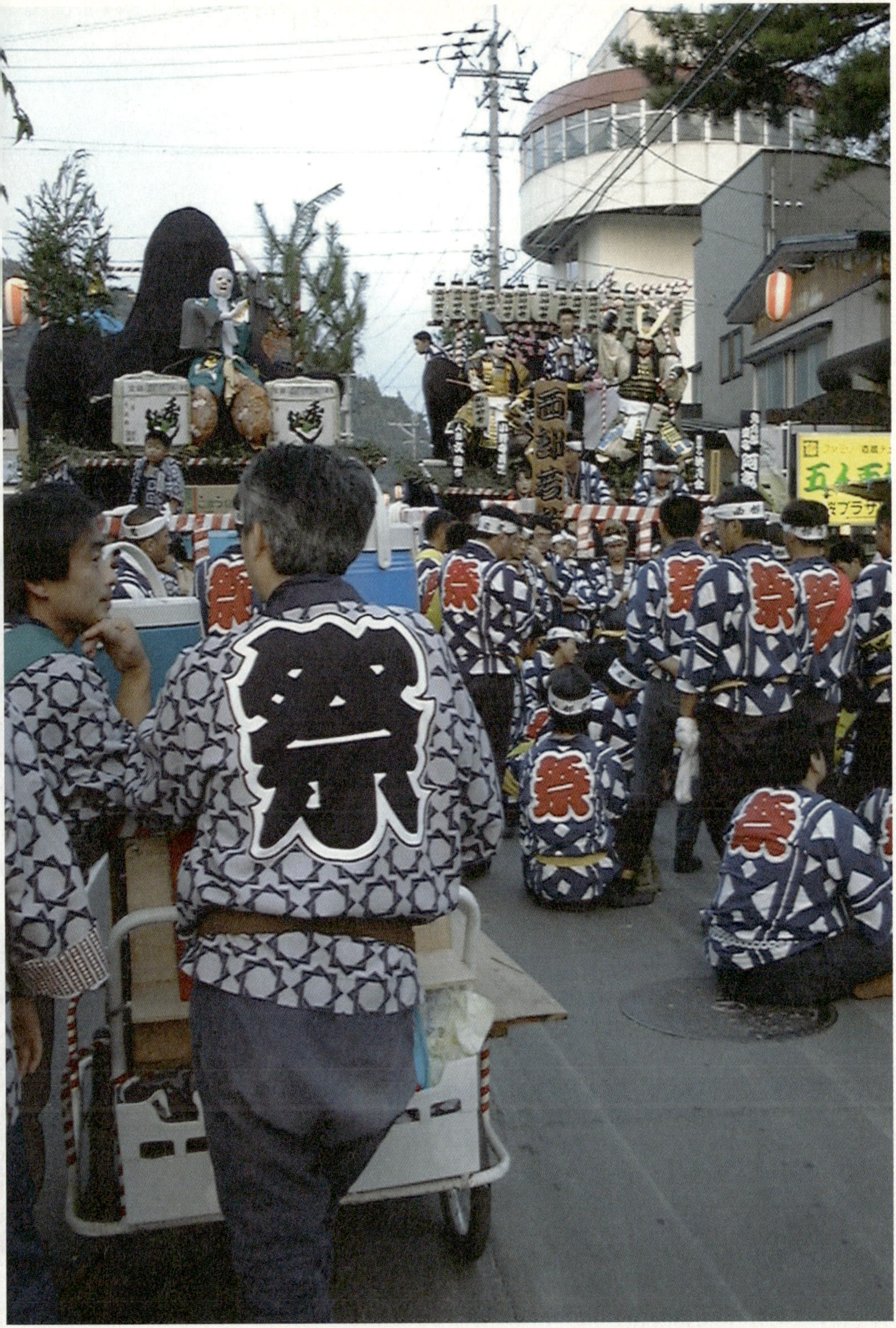
祭

夢があろうとなかろうと、楽しく生きてる奴が最強。

Have a dream or not,
those that are enjoying life are the strongest.

自由を求めることなく、
自由を叫ぶことなく、
さりげなく、自由に生きればいい。

Not in search of freedom
Not crying out for freedom
Just live casually and freely

自分の愛するもののために。
そして、自分を愛してくれるもののために。

ただ、まっすぐ、まっすぐ。

for the one you love
and, for the one that loves you

straight...just...straight

すべては、自分が選んでる。

You choose everything

自分の心の声に正直に。

be true to the voice in your heart

LOVE & FREE

この本の誕生に関わったすべての人に感謝します。

特に、デザイナーであり、弟であるミノルに。
彼の存在自体が、旅先での自分の励みになっていた。

そして、「マザー二瓶」こと、二瓶 明に。
彼のアシストがなかったら、何も始まらなかったし、何も終わらなかった。

最後に、サヤカへ。
「いつも、ありがとう！」

I'd like to thank each and every person that was involved in making this book come to life.

Especially, to my younger brother, MINORU, who designed the book. His existence, itself, was encouragement throughout my journey.

And also to "Mother NIHEI"-Akira Nihei.
Without his assistance, nothing would have started, and nothing would have finished.

Finally, to Sayaka.
Thank you, always!

この作品は2001年3月に小社より刊行された「LOVE&FREE」にバイリンガル版として新たに英文を加え、デザインを一新したものです。

著者紹介

高橋歩　http://www.ayumu.ch/

作家・自由人。
(株) A-Works、(株) play earth、(株) アイランドプロジェクト代表取締役。
A-Works, Inc. : http://www.a-works.gr.jp
Island Project, Inc . : http://www.shimapro.com

1972年、東京都生まれ。20歳のとき、映画『カクテル』に憧れ、大学を中退、仲間とアメリカンバー「ROCKWELL'S」を開店。2年間で4店舗に広げ、店の仲間を中心に「サークルHEAVEN」を設立。「死んだらごめんツアー」と呼ばれるギリギリのイベントを多数開催するが、運良く、死なず。23歳のとき、自伝を出すために仲間と「サンクチュアリ出版」を設立。数々のヒット作をプロデュース。自伝の『毎日が冒険』もベストセラーを記録。26歳で結婚。結婚式の3日後、すべての肩書きをリセットし、妻とふたりで世界一周の大冒険に出かける。約2年間で北極から南極まで、世界数十カ国を放浪の末、帰国。2000年12月、沖縄へ移住。仲間と「〜カフェバー＆海辺の宿〜ビーチロックハウス」をオープン。現在は沖縄に住み、二児の父親として子育てに燃焼しながら、東京とニューヨークにオフィスを持つ出版を中心としたファクトリー「A-Works」、世界中に飲食店を展開する「play earth」、沖縄に音楽と冒険とアートの溢れるアイランドビレッジを創る「アイランドプロジェクト」の代表として活動中。執筆活動や全国でのトークライブ（講演）も行っている。
著書に、『人生の地図』『アドベンチャーライフ』『ワールドジャーニー』『サンクチュアリ』など多数。

With a new design and the addition of English translations, this is the renewed billingual version of Love & Free which was originally published in March, 2001.

About the Author

Ayumu Takahashi : www.ayumu.ch

Author & "Free Man"
President, A-Works, Inc.; play earth, Inc.; Island Project, Inc.
A-Works, Inc. : http://www.a-works.gr.jp
Island Project, Inc . : http://www.shimapro.com

Born in Tokyo, Japan, in 1972. At the age of twenty, inspired by the movie *Cocktail*, dropped out of college, and opened an American bar, "Rockwell's" with his friends. In two years, he expanded to 4 bars, and established "Circle Heaven" centered around his friends from his bars. Events called "Sorry If We Die Tours" were held, but luckily, no one died.

At the age of 23, in order to publish an autobiography, he established Sanctuary Publishing, Inc., with his friends, and produced a number of hits. His autobiography *Everyday is an Adventure* recorded as a bestseller. He married at 26. Three days after the wedding, he reset all his titles, and set out on a journey around the world with his wife. In approximately two years, from the North Pole to the South Pole, after roaming thirty-some countries around the world, he returned home. In December, 2000, he settled in Okinawa. And with his friends opened Café & Beach Inn: Beach Rock House. Presently, while living in Okinawa, exerting himself to fathering his two children; he is active as president of A-Works, Inc., a publishing-centered factory in Tokyo and New York City; play earth, Inc., that develops restaurants and bars around the world; and Island Project, Inc., that is building a village filled with music, adventure, and art, in Okinawa.

He also actively writes and conducts "Live Talks."

Among his many works include *The Map of Life, Adventure Life, World Journey, and Sanctuary*.

LOVE & FREE NEW YORK EDITION
WORDS & PHOTOS collected from the streets around the world

2006年3月25日 初版発行（2008年4月に一部改訂）
2011年6月10日 第8刷発行

写真・文	高橋歩
デザイン	横田直人（from UN）/ 高橋実
編集・制作	磯尾克行 / 滝本洋平
アシスタント	森木妙子 / 大津祐子
翻 訳	みっしぇる・どすたー
アドバイザー	リッキー・トム
アシスタント	藤森美紀子

発行者　鶴巻謙介

発行・発売　サンクチュアリ出版
東京都渋谷区千駄ヶ谷2-38-1　〒151-0051
TEL：03-5775-5192　FAX：03-5775-5193
URL：http://www.sanctuarybooks.jp/　E-mail：info@sanctuarybooks.jp

印刷・製本　中央精版印刷株式会社

©Ayumu Takahashi　※本書の無断複写・複製・転載を禁じます。
落丁本、乱丁本は送料小社負担にてお取替えいたします。
ISBN978-4-86113-916-1

LOVE & FREE NEW YORK EDITION
WORDS & PHOTOS collected from the streets around the world

Library of Congress Control Number: 2007943895
copyright　©Ayumu Takahashi
ALL RIGHTS RESERVED

No part of this book may be reproduced or transmitted in any form or by any means, electronic or mechanical, including photocopying, recording, or by any information storage and retrieval system, without the written permission of the publisher. For information contact One Peace Books Inc.

WORDS & PHOTOS　AYUMU TAKAHASHI

DESIGNER	NAOTO YOKOTA (from UN) & MINORU TAKAHASHI
EDITOR	KATSUYUKI ISOO & YOUHEI TAKIMOTO
ASSISTANT	TAEKO MORIKI & YUKO OTSU
TRANSLATOR	MICHELLE DOSTER
ADVISER	RICKY TOM
ASSISTANT	MIKIKO FUJIMORI

Published by One Peace Books Inc.., New York, New York

One Peace Books Inc.
57 GREAT JONES STREET, NEW YORK, NY 10012 USA
TEL：212-260-4400　FAX：212-995-2969
URL：http://www.onepeacebooks.com

PRINTED IN JAPAN